Haute Cuisine Without Help

HAUTE CUISINE WITHOUT HELP

Harold Knapik

LIVERIGHT
New York

Standard Book Number: 87140-526-1
Library of Congress Catalog Card Number: 70-131271

1.987654321

DESIGNED BY BETTY BINNS

Manufactured in the United States of America

THIS BOOK IS DEDICATED TO

MY WIFE, VIRGINIA, TO THE

MEMORY OF ALICE B. TOKLAS,

AND TO THE REMEMBRANCES OF

THE WONDERFUL TIMES AND MEALS

WE ENJOYED TOGETHER IN PARIS

AND IN THE SOUTH OF FRANCE,

DURING WHAT NOW SOMETIMES

SEEMS TO ME TO HAVE BEEN

ANOTHER LIFE

1561142

CONTENTS

CONTENTS

INTRODUCTION

I HAVE been cooking for over twenty-five years now, twelve of them in France. Only a blithering idiot could live in Paris that long and not learn something about food. I not only wanted to learn, I was avidly curious, and since, in France, everyone from a member of the *Académie française* to one's concierge is expert and articulate about food, I did learn. The French orientation of my cooking, however, was formed long before I got to France. One of the two books I carried with me through four years of World War II was *Ma Cuisine* by Auguste Escoffier; the other was James Joyce's

Ulysses. Reading them and rereading them, which I perforce had to do, sustained me.

When my wife and I went to Paris in 1948, we were fortunate in the people we met, but no doubt the most attractive and forceful person we came to know intimately was Alice B. Toklas. I remember our first meeting very well. We were staying with friends in Chantilly, some ninety kilometers to the north of Paris and notable for its exclusive devotion to horses and horse racing—the race track and training meadows are larger than the town. Alice and a friend came for lunch. In the absence of a reliable cook, my wife and I volunteered to do the cooking. The meal was not at all bad and Alice was kind in her compliments on the first courses. However, when it came to the dessert, a sumptuous and gooey combination of sponge cake, fresh raspberries, cream, and a liqueur, she became quite enthusiastic and asked if I had made it. I acknowledged I had, and she murmured, "the courage of youth." In 1948 it took a bit of doing to rustle up ingredients such as butter and cream, but this was simplified for us because my wife worked at the American Embassy in Paris, which maintained a fine commissary in its basement that helped all its employees in the early postwar years. After all, it was illegal in France in 1948 to sell anything resembling real white bread; croissants were but a prewar memory. I did manage to buy some black market croissants while we were in Chantilly, and they were the best I have ever tasted. The price I paid for them could very well have kept my memory green.

Not long after that first meeting, we were invited to lunch with Alice at her apartment at 5 rue Christine— the first of many memorable lunches—and it gave me a good idea of the culinary league I aspired to. Later, beginning in 1950, we took our vacations with Alice every summer. We would rent a furnished villa in the south of France, get there by plane, car, or train, unpack our bags, reconnoiter the neighborhood for shops, and then plan our first meal. Alice's only formal meal of her day—and ours, while on vacation—was lunch, a leisurely affair of at least two hours, which does not mean that vast quantities of food were consumed; we just took our time. In the beginning Alice and I took turns cooking, but, in a household of three, two cooks were too many—especially two temperamental cooks. So Alice, who did all her own cooking in Paris, decided to really have a vacation and left the cooking to me. Good food was cheap and one day, halfway through a vacation, I added up our accounts and announced that we were eating for such and such a sum—a very low one. Alice was appalled and promptly made reservations for lunch for all of us at the two most expensive restaurants in the region.

Perhaps the principal reasons for the current interest in cooking, especially for buffet-style dining, are the unavailability of adequate hired help, a shortage of good caterers, the high price of all caterers, and the deficiencies of most restaurants. Since the absence of qualified hired help is compounded by an even greater lack of training in such help as is available, we might just as well settle down to doing the best we can on our own. This, as I mean to show in this book, can be very rewarding. Cooking doesn't merely mean work; it is a most pleasurable and useful hobby. It can be therapeutic in the sense that gardening is, and since, ideally, one cooks for someone or for others, there is a nice unselfishness about it. In any case, I have no doubt that with a degree of application and experience and a modicum of talent, you can do as well as, or better than, most restaurants and caterers. For example, you are not, as restaurants are, required by the exigencies of time and the high cost of good chefs either to ignore vegetables or to cook them in such a fashion that their flavors evoke only the faintest suggestion of what they should be.

Quite aside from the quality of restaurant food are its astonishing prices. The French have a saying that luxury has no price—a sentiment with which I agree—but since haute cuisine hardly exists in American restaurants today, we are obliged to regard it as an unpurchasable luxury. Although restaurateurs do not serve mediocre food by choice, there are those who wouldn't recognize good food if they tasted it, and almost all restaurateurs come to terms too quickly with the dubious advantages of institutional-type prepared and precooked foods. I am not referring only to restaurant vegetables, about which the less said the better.

Many of the recipes in this book are easy—almost foolproof—and this is so indicated; others are moderately difficult, and a few are very difficult. I would like to stress the value of puff paste, which has so many uses as well as the faculty of raising even simple dishes to splendor. For example, no one takes an apple tart made with puff paste for granted, and a fillet of beef in a puff-paste crust is certainly something more than an ordinary roast of beef. Try the foolproof recipe for puff paste on page 227; I don't believe you will be disappointed.

The pâtés in this book also deserve emphasis, not only because of their flavor but also because of their marvelous compactness. When sliced properly thin for buffet serving, a five-pound pâté can easily serve forty guests, accompanied by other food, of course, and provided that some errant eaters do not sail into it under the impression that it is meat loaf. Pâtés of the sort given in this book are not rich, except in flavor; the fat essential to their cooking is gently pressed out before the pâtés become firm, leaving only the lean meat and the juices.

A third item I wish to stress is the basic sauce given on page 19. It is not hard to make and, while its preparation takes time, the inconvenience is more than balanced by the finished product—a very reduced essence, unobtainable commercially, which is used only in small quantities. A typical batch of it makes up to two quarts or more. A few tablespoons added to, say, the pan juices of a *steak au poivre* or a veal cutlet lifts the dish to the category of la haute cuisine. Try making it over a lazy weekend.

I know a very bright twenty-one-year-old girl who is so interested in French cooking that she and her fiancé, who is equally interested, enthusiastically but methodically have dinner at least once a week in one of the better New York French restaurants. After each meal they make a note of what they have eaten and drunk. They are not hesitant to try unfamiliar dishes. One day the girl saw on my desk a culinary *aide mémoire* written by one of Escoffier's pupils and asked if she could borrow it. A few days later, somewhat crestfallen, she returned it to me saying, "I thought I could get something from this book, but I now realize that it would take years to really know my way around in the French cuisine." The book did list over 200 recipes for consommé and over 150 for omelets, and these were but a small fraction of the contents.

One may well ask if the complexity of the French cuisine is necessary. The only reasonable answer is that it just came about that way. It is no more easily explained than is why so many symphonies were written in Vienna. It may be because in foodstuffs and wines, the French have more of everything than anyone else. The only other national cuisines that approach the

French in quality and range are the Italian and the Chinese. The Italians have little beef and indifferent fowl. The Chinese also have little beef and, for the most part, do not eat lamb or mutton; their favorite meat is pork. The Italians have some excellent cheeses, but nothing comparable to the best of French cheeses. The Chinese have no cheese at all—or any other dairy products for that matter. The Italians have a limited number of good desserts, but their pastry cannot match that of the French. Chinese desserts are insignificant. The Italians have some good wines, but none that approach the best of French wines. Chinese wines are inferior. Having noted what her rivals are weak in, I might list those things unique to the cuisine of France. Without going into great detail, I can mention: *foie gras*, *belons* and *marennes* oysters, salt marsh lamb (*pré-salé*), Charolais beef, *poulets et poulardes de Bresse*, magnificent crustaceans and fish, the blackest and most pungent of truffles, the one and only cognac, an immense variety of vegetables, and incomparable fruit, ranging from the *calville* apples of Normandy to the lemons of the district around Menton. Italian cooks are superb, possibly the most imaginative of all, but they do not have the materials available to French chefs. That the Italians have a flair for cooking is evident in the number who are expert in the French cuisine; they turn up all over the world, and there are a good many of them in France—especially Paris, although London has the most. Chinese chefs are certainly inventive, but the ingredients available in China are somewhat limited. Incidentally, the French, who are chauvinistic about their cuisine, are nevertheless enthusiastic about Italian and Chinese food. Paris has many foreign restaurants, including several Czech restaurants, one of which must be the best Czech restaurant in the world today.

Alice Toklas wasn't much interested in the analytical approach to food. She made this clear in her often repeated remark, "It was calories in World War I and vitamins in World War II." She pronounced the first syllable of vitamins to rhyme with sit, which made a preoccupation with them seem inane. However, since Alice couldn't have weighed more than ninety pounds and never gained so much as an ounce, she could afford to ignore calories; the vitamins were easily taken care of because she loved fruit and vegetables. Few of us are so fortunate; and while good cooking has nothing to do with dieting, an unrelieved diet of *la haute cuisine* would be catastrophic for one's health and, even sadder, eventually boring.

The last time I had lunch at Le Grand Vefour in Paris, I noticed an interesting item on the menu: *boeuf bourguignon*. Without going into the question of how a Burgundian dish had insinuated itself into a bastion of Bordeaux food and wine, one might wonder what place this rustic dish had in a three-star restaurant. The answer is simple: Le Grand Vefour, whose prices are quite as high as its cuisine is *haute*, nevertheless has a good many regular customers (in my time, Colette and Cocteau, both of whom lived in the same building as the restaurant), and *boeuf bourguignon* is one of those dishes that Frenchmen become nostalgic about, especially when their livers are acting up. Putting it on the menu is a nice gesture on the part of the management. This underlines what I set out to say: The difference between the highest category of French cooking and the lesser orders is mainly a matter of richness and elaborateness of preparation, although obviously the more modest restaurants also use more modest ingredients. For example, on the rue Royale in Paris, which is one block long, there used to be three remarkable restau-

rants, all on the same side of the street, Maxim at one
end, Larue at the other end, and almost exactly in the
middle, Weber. Maxim (the only one of the three still
in operation) and Larue represented *la haute cuisine*—
magnificent quality, flawless preparation and presentation, great wines, impeccable service, and very high
prices. Weber, which was what the French call *un
maison classique*, was less luxurious in decor than its
neighbors and much, much more reasonable in its
prices, but it served excellent food, cooked in an un-
complicated manner. *Sole Albert*, one of the specialties
of Maxim, is not to be taken for granted, but neither
was the grilled sole with *sauce tartare* at Weber. In fact,
the quality of the fish in both houses was undoubtedly
identical—a fact that, as far as I am concerned, is crucial. My point then is that no matter what you serve,
whether it be a fried egg or *poularde Albufera*, a toasted
slice of bread or a fresh croissant, there should always
be present and apparent the characteristics of good
cooking: high-quality ingredients, careful preparation,
and pleasing presentation.

Cookbook writers insist on using the word *dramatic*
to describe what they believe to be particularly effective
presentations of food. The only meals I have ever been
served that could reasonably be called dramatic were
spectacular flops (the French word *raté*, which means
more or less the same thing, has the right ring). Of
course, a lot of the drama on these occasions took place
in the kitchen and, what with tears and muffled curses,
adequately filled the bill. The guests, while making the
grimaces that pass for smiles on such occasions, must
attempt the impossible—to conceal a large piece of
something inedible by placing it under a smaller piece
of something innocuous, such as a potato. I actually
licked this problem once in a restaurant in the south
of France. I went to a local restaurant alone (Alice and

my wife Virginia had gone off to visit Pablo Picasso)
and, as Alice put it, I was nobly casing the restaurant's
cuisine with the view to our giving it further custom if
it turned out to be good. For the first course I ordered
a poached trout. So far so good. My choice for the
second course was steak, and it was inedible. Since I
detest making a fuss in restaurants, I panicked for a
moment. However, I remembered that I had brought
with me a copy of the local newspaper, *Nice Matin,*
and it gave me an idea. I waited, and it took a while,
until the over-solicitous waiter and the other customers
were occupied and quickly slid the steak into the folds
of the newspaper. My plan worked, although the waiter
did give a start when he saw my empty plate. On my
way home with the paper and steak tucked under my
arm, I easily imagined the story he would tell about
the American *carnivore* who had devoured a large steak,
including all the fat and gristle, in what must have been
two bites. One of our neighbors, a cat, enjoyed the steak
very much.

I remember a dinner party that could have been
dramatic, but the drama involved a drink rather than
food. The setting was Paris; the occasion, Christmas
Eve. The American host, one of the embassy crowd, was
going to treat his guests to a before-dinner drink he had
heard about that required igniting whiskey—the chief
ingredient in the concoction he proposed. As the treat
was slow in coming and thinking I might be able to
help, I ambled into the foyer where he was preparing
the mixture. When I reached him, the host was pouring
100-proof bourbon into a receptacle just a bit smaller
than a washtub, which was almost full. He then lit a
match and, when I saw that he meant to put it to the
liquid, I managed to dissuade him. It turned out that
since he had been having difficulty igniting the potion,
he thought it needed more whiskey. He then, as I sug-

gested, heated a relatively small quantity in a pot and put a match to it. It lit all right—and with a blast—the flame hitting the ceiling. Except for a good dinner, the remainder of the evening was uneventful.

I have seen all sorts of charts, tables, and so-called handy guides that purportedly settle once and for all the tricky business of what herb or spice, and how much of it, should be used for any given dish. This is so much bilge. It is not that easy; nothing resembling a blanket formula will work.

The one standard combination of herbs, the *bouquet garni* of the French cuisine—bay leaf, thyme in sprigs, and parsley—is a tried-and-true blend that imparts just the right earthy flavor to countless dishes, but even it is not treated in an offhand manner. When a *bouquet garni* is indicated, the recipe should state the size—small, medium, or large. A small *bouquet garni* consists of a piece of bay leaf the size of a dime, a sprig of parsley, and a small sprig of thyme. In Spain, where everything is a little more so, the markets in the Mediterranean towns sell hefty *bouquets* that the fishermen use to flavor their soup. A familiar sight of the Costa Brava is that of a barefoot fisherman walking toward the beach, swinging a well-tied bundle of herbs and greens. One day as I was walking home from the market with one of these bundles, I heard an English woman say to her husband, "Who says there are no blond Catalonians?"

Alice Toklas attributed the post-World War II popularity of herbs and spices in France to the need during the German occupation to reinforce the flavor of meat, which was, to put it mildly, in short supply. With due respect, I don't agree with that and for good reason. Alice had a heavy hand with herbs and didn't really like or understand spices, which reminds me of her first attempt to make *rouille*—a Provençal sauce, properly made with *poivre doux d'Espagne* (a sort of Spanish paprika) and olive oil, thickened with bread crumbs or egg yolks, and mounted like a mayonnaise. Alice had tasted *rouille* for the first time when Picasso took us to lunch at Juan-les-Pins. The lunch was excellent, and Picasso demonstrated his enthusiasm for the *rouille* (which, although intended to accompany the broiled lobsters we had ordered, had been placed on the table the moment we were seated) by dipping pieces of bread into it and then into freshly grated Gruyère cheese that was also on the table. He devoured the morsels of his improvised hors d'oeuvre with great relish. In any case, when we were back in Paris after vacation, Alice dropped in one evening and announced that she had served *rouille* to an American guest for lunch that day. I don't recall the name of the guest, but I think of him from time to time, because Alice had made her *rouille* with cayenne pepper.

My wife and I have lived in New York since 1961 and have learned that cooking can be as much fun here as it was in Paris. You don't have to be French to cook well. Certain ingredients that were lacking in 1961 are now available. The culinary situation at this point can only be called excellent, *if* you know how to cook. If you must depend on restaurants, all I can do is wish you luck.

I have taught cooking, but never for a fee; my pupils are my friends. At the head of my list, I unhesitatingly place the Dr. Gary Johnsons. He was our friend before he married, and his wife Judy became our friend and my pupil. Eventually Gary became interested in cooking and wines, and after nine years of dedicated application to enjoying ourselves with cooking and eating, we are now all cooks together.

Haute Cuisine Without Help

UTENSILS

IT IS impossible to cook well unless you have at hand the necessary utensils, and I admit that this runs into money. Therefore, young people setting up house should be careful to buy only what is genuinely useful; a *batterie de cuisine* (everything that is used in the kitchen in the way of utensils) can be built up gradually. There is only one rule that applies to purchases: buy the best. A good omelet pan will last more than a lifetime, as will a good mortar and pestle made of marble or porcelain. In fact, unless they are abused, these utensils can last for a hundred years. I have rented furnished villas in the south of France that had such items in the kitchen, and I appreciated them for their serviceability as well as their age. The following items would seem to me to be basic to any kitchen.

Omelet Pan

An omelet pan, preferably of cast-iron, can be used for frying eggs and making crepes as well as omelets, but don't fry bacon or anything else in it. It should not be washed in water, but cleaned well with paper towels. If you believe there is something of a myth about this sort of pan, forget it; it is a reality.

Knives

Knives of carbon steel are the only general-purpose knives worth having. However, the qualification *general-purpose* is used expressly, because for certain procedures a stainless steel knife is excellent. For instance (and contrary to what some have been led to believe), for slicing eggplant or cutting up fruit, slicing eggs or cleaning fish, a stainless steel knife with a serrated blade and sharp edge is best, and they now manage to manufacture such knives with edges that remain sharp for a considerable length of time. Why do you suppose they use ivory spoons for handling caviar? And have you ever experienced what carbon steel can do to the flavor of a sardine?

Incidentally, keeping knives sharp is no great task. Using the blunt side of a carbon steel knife as the sharpener or stone, sweep the blade of the knife you wish to sharpen up and across in a motion away from you, against the sharpener, turning the knife from time to time so that each side is sharpened.

Above all you should have a French-type chopping knife (*couteau à mincer*) with a carbon steel blade. This is the true all-purpose knife. It is usually about thirteen and one-half inches long and straight across the top. The blade is slanted in such a way that, by manipulating the handle while holding the tip of the knife with the other hand, one can chop just about anything very swiftly. Items chopped this way are superior to those chopped in any sort of chopping apparatus. The mechanical choppers do not cut as well as they crush, and the texture of the results are very different.

Large Pot

A large, heavy-bottomed pot (a five- or six-quart one) will turn out to have more uses than you can imagine. It can serve for making soup, boiling beef, or poaching a chicken; it is absolutely essential in making the basic sauce given in this book (see p. 19).

Frying Pan

A large, heavy *sautoir*, or frying pan, with high sides for sautéing meat or vegetables will have unlimited service. If the indication that heaviness is desirable in pots strikes you as repetitive, allow me to point out the reason for the insistence on weight: Foods cooked in a heavy pot are not likely to burn, and with such a pot you can cook stews or sautés (they should be covered with foil or a lid) on a gas or electric burner on top of the stove with a result not inferior to the same dish cooked in the oven.

Spoon

A perforated spoon is handy for many things, such as draining and serving poached eggs, testing pasta or draining lasagna, and removing meat from a sauce that needs straining. A stainless steel spoon is best; enameled ones tend to lose bits of their enamel, which renders them unsightly as well as unsanitary.

Small Pots

Two-quart and three-quart pots are essential for boiling vegetables and making sauces, among many other uses. Buy stainless steel (preferably with a copper bottom) or glass pots, as they do not impart a metallic flavor to foods. Glass pots are ideal for poaching eggs.

Skillet

A skillet of heavy aluminum or stainless steel with very low, hardly noticeable, sides can be used for pan broiling, cooking bacon, frying potatoes (see p. 201), and cooking anything crisply. High sides produce steam, which for a steak, for example, would be disastrous.

Bowl

A copper bowl is best for beating egg whites (there is one designed expressly for that purpose). It can usually be bought in shops that specialize in French utensils or sometimes through mail-order houses. However, except for a factor too subtle to go into—the properties of copper in relation to egg whites and sugar—a large porcelain bowl will do very well. The porcelain bowl can be used for many other dishes; the copper bowl cannot. For example, a copper bowl would not get along with the lemon in a salad.

Whisk

A wire whisk, as almost everyone knows, is ideal for beating egg whites. Using a whisk, however, demands a certain technique—especially a suppleness of wrist—which everyone does not have. A hand-held electric beater can also do a very good job, especially if it is manipulated in a round, over-and-under movement.

Blender

A blender is almost a necessity today. No one has the time to work with sieves, and a blender will puree even the skins of peas for a soup—a feat not previously possible. When used carefully (and its use can be overdone) the blender is probably the most important new element in cooking. However, since it tends to reduce everything to pablum if allowed to—and this is the key —care has to be exercised in its use. It is possible, especially with the better blenders, to blend to a degree and not to oblivion, but only experience and judgment can help here.

Colander

A colander is a necessity for draining salad, pasta, vegetables, poached fruit, rice for salad, and many other foods. Buy a good one, preferably enameled; it will stand you in good stead.

Potato Peeler

Potato peelers are useful for more than peeling potatoes—for example, asparagus, carrots, white turnips, cucumbers, zucchini, the zest of lemon—and they do a very good job. Buy the kind that is not rigid, that has a movable blade.

SOUPS

SOUP, one of the most delicious, wholesome, and attractive foods, is certainly the most flexible; there are soups for every taste, appetite, occasion, season, climate, and, for that matter, time of day. However, with the variety of frozen, canned, and dehydrated soups on the market, homemade soup has become something of a rarity, and that, I feel, is a pity. It does take more effort to make homemade soup than it does to open a can or a package, but the results are not at all comparable. And since soup freezes very well and the effort required to make it diminishes in direct ratio to the quantity made, plan a large batch which can be frozen and spaced out for serving over a period of months. Making your own soups provides the opportunity to use seasonal vegetables when they are fresh and cost least.

May I add that all soups need not be hearty or have the quality of "sticking to the ribs." Aside from the melancholy fact that food that sticks to the ribs is likely to stick elsewhere, there are times for a robust soup and times for a delicate one, with many gradations in between. To know which to serve when is a demonstration of culinary intuition.

POTAGE MIMOSA

Potage mimosa is a garnished bouillon or consommé. Its garnish of sliced green beans and egg yolks, hard-boiled and forced through a large-holed sieve, actually evokes mimosa, and its flavor has something of the simple freshness of that flowering tree.

INGREDIENTS FOR EIGHT

8 cups chicken or beef bouillon

1 package frozen French-cut green beans

2 hard-boiled eggs (only the yolks)

salt and pepper

To make: Cook the beans in very little water until just done. Do not overcook. If the beans are too long, cut them in half. Hard-boil the eggs, chill them, peel, and remove the whites. Heat the bouillon. Force the egg yolks into the bouillon through a large-holed sieve. Add the drained beans.

[8]

To serve: Mix lightly and serve. This makes a fine light dinner soup.

SOUPE AU PISTOU

Soupe au pistou, as anyone acquainted with it never fails to mention, is of Genoese origin—a bit of information that contributes nothing toward an understanding of the soup. The Genoese soups that include *pesto* (a flavoring mixture identical to that used in this soup) are minestrone varieties that involve a large number of vegetables, including cabbage and dried beans. Authentic French *soupe au pistou* is made only with fresh green beans, fresh tomatoes, potatoes, garlic, olive oil, fresh basil, grated cheese, and noodles. No onion, meat, or meat stock is used, which makes it highly individual. *Pistou* is the Provençal word for *pesto*, the Italian word which translated into English is *pestle*. This is of even less help. In the south of France, the common name for basil (*basilic*) is *pistou*; in other words, the name of the utensil is given to the essential ingredient of the soup—the basil.

Soupe au pistou is a simple soup; in fact, it out-simplifies and out-tastes any other. It has such delicacy and measure that my wife (a basil addict) and I felt real regret at the prospect of foregoing it in New York. We didn't then know that Italian shops in New York and a large number of other cities handle fresh basil in season, but we did better than relying on shops. By bulldozing friends into growing basil in their gardens or on their terraces and growing it in our window boxes, even through the winter, we have enjoyed a series of *pistou* meals of a quality that would startle a native of Saint-Tropez. We enhance the soup by using homemade noodles.

INGREDIENTS FOR SIX

1½ lb (cleaned weight) tender green beans, cleaned and cut into ¾ inch pieces (Frozen green beans of the best quality may be used, and the French-cut variety are excellent.)

4 large tomatoes, peeled, seeded, and chopped (The tomatoes must be very ripe. If the only kind available is the pink blotting-paper type, use a 28-ounce can of plum tomatoes.)

4 medium potatoes (Use a variety that does not crumble; for example, do not use Idaho potatoes.)

2 large handfuls fresh basil (Use only the leaves.)

3 to 6 cloves garlic, peeled

½ cup, or more, first-quality olive oil

1 cup each Switzerland Swiss and Parmesan cheese, freshly grated and thoroughly mixed

salt and pepper

noodles, preferably homemade (Any good quality, not-too-thin, commercial noodle will do, but they should not be much over one inch in length. Since some people like more noodles than others, it is best to cook them separately and serve them that way, putting them in the soup plates and pouring the soup over them. You should have at least ½ cup of cooked noodles per person.)

To make: Put the green beans, tomatoes, potatoes, salt, and pepper into about three quarts of water. (The liquid content of this soup varies with preference, but the soup should not be too thin.) Bring to a boil and cook over fairly high heat (about 400°) until the beans are two-thirds done. If you wish to cook the noodles in the soup, add them at this point; otherwise continue cooking the soup until the beans are just tender. Do not overcook the beans or noodles.

While the soup cooks, pound two large handfuls of fresh basil in a fairly large mortar with the peeled garlic and the olive oil. The result should be a smooth amalgam. (Although the texture, and consequently the flavor, will not be quite the same, you can puree the mixture in a food-mill or a blender. If you use a blender, mix at low speed just until fairly smooth.) When the soup is done and boiling hot, pour the contents of the mortar into the soup, swishing some soup in the mortar—or whatever vessel you use—to pick up all the sauce. Stir and serve with the grated cheese separately.

Note: In order to effect a proper blending, the soup must be boiling when the mixture of oil and basil is added. *Bouillabaisse*, which involves a mixture of oil and stock, is also cooked over very high heat to achieve this sort of blending.

HOMEMADE NOODLES FOR SOUP

The flavor of homemade noodles is so superior to any commercial noodle that I ask you to try this recipe. The dough is not only useful for soup noodles but is the prototype for everything from *fettucini* to lasagne, and by extension, to such dishes as Siberian *pelmeny* and Afghanistan stuffed dough pockets. The noodles are also excellent served as a garnish with meat stews, fricassees, braised meats, or even roasts, when mixed with sour cream or bread crumbs sautéed in butter.

[1 1]

INGREDIENTS FOR SIX

3 eggs, lightly beaten

3 cups white all-purpose flour (approximate measure)

1 tsp butter, melted

½ tsp salt, or more

Note: It isn't practical to give the precise quantity of flour required to make this dough. Some flours absorb more liquid than others, eggs vary in size, and, most to the point, some cooks have stronger hands than others and can incorporate more flour into the eggs, which is desirable if you like firm noodles.

To make: The method is simplicity itself. Mix the eggs, butter, and salt in a large bowl. Add flour a little at a time, blending constantly with a fork until the dough is dry enough to knead by hand. Then throw the dough on a floured table or board and, with all the strength you have, incorporate flour into it, little by little, squeezing, pulling, and pounding until the mass is of even texture and very firm. Cover the dough with a bowl and set it aside for thirty minutes.

Next, divide the dough into three pieces (or two, if you have a large rolling space) and roll each piece out until very thin. Allow sheets of dough to dry for ten minutes, dust them with flour, roll them up like jelly rolls, and with a sharp knife slice them as thin or as thick as you wish. In gauging the thickness of the noodles you want, don't forget that they swell up considerably during the cooking process.

In a colander, wash excess flour off the uncooked

noodles and throw them into a large pot of salted boiling water. Test them after five or six minutes. Homemade noodles take much less time to cook than commercial noodles, and they should be drained while still slightly tough. They will continue to cook for a few minutes in the heat they retain. Do not rinse in cold water.

FRESH GREEN PEA SOUP

This is a version of the French classic, *Potage Saint-Germain*, but it is an improved, not a so-called convenient or downgraded one. It cannot, however, be made without a blender. A blender purees the pea skins as well as the pulp and converts them into a velvety pale-green cream--a result impossible to achieve with a sieve or vegetable-mill, however fine. And, the process takes only a few minutes and no effort with a blender, as compared to at least thirty minutes and a good deal of work with a sieve or mill. Some people say this treatment produces a puree rather similar to baby food. My only answer is that if baby food tasted like this pea soup, I would eat it with pleasure.

INGREDIENTS FOR SIX TO EIGHT

2 packages best-quality frozen peas

6 to 8 cups chicken stock, preferably homemade (This soup made with canned chicken stock will be very tasty, but not as fine as if made with homemade stock.)

4 Tbsp sour cream

salt and white pepper

To make: Cook the peas in stock until just done and puree them in batches in a blender with enough of the stock to liquify the mixture. Use the blender at slow speed and just long enough to puree the peas. Add some of the sour cream to each batch just before turning off the blender. Mix the puree with the remaining stock until it is just the thickness you want. Add salt and pepper before serving.

To serve: Reheat it and that's all there is to it—except to experience the extraordinary flavor. This soup is also wonderful chilled with a garnish of finely chopped chives, parsley, mint, or chervil, but the herbs must be fresh.

SOUP OF SALAD GREENS

I usually make this soup when my wife and I want to serve a good mixed salad. We like a mixture of Bibb and Simpson lettuce, romaine, escarole, chicory, and watercress. Since the tender inside leaves of these greens (not the watercress) are best for salad and the outer, greener but tougher leaves are best for soup, it works out just right. Although we make a lot of soup, it freezes well.

INGREDIENTS FOR EIGHT

½ *large head Simpson lettuce*

½ *head Bibb lettuce*

½ *head romaine*

½ *head escarole*

½ *head chicory*

½ *bunch watercress (including stems)*

1 medium (17-ounce) can plum tomatoes, forced through a sieve

1 medium carrot, chopped fine

1 bunch scallions (including half the green parts), chopped fine

1 handful parsley (leaves and stems), roughly chopped

2 leek (with one-third the green part), finely chopped

1 stalk celery (with leaves), finely chopped

4 cups beef or chicken stock or bouillon

½ *tsp dried basil*

salt and pepper

3 medium potatoes, peeled and chopped

4 Tbsp butter or oil

To make: Heat the butter or oil in a thick-bottomed pot. Add the carrot, scallions, leek, celery, and potatoes and sauté over low heat for fifteen minutes, stirring frequently. Then add all the other ingredients with enough of the bouillon to wilt the greens which, to begin with, are voluminous, but reduce rapidly. If

[15]

necessary, add the greens a bit at a time. When they have wilted, add the rest of the bouillon and enough water to cover the greens well. Cook for one hour over lowest heat. Do not cover the pot.

The next step is best with a blender, but a food-mill will do. Place another large pot near the stove. Batch by batch, mix the soup in the blender and pour each blended batch into the clean pot. Do not overblend the mixture; it should be just pureed, not aerated. If the soup is too thick, add stock or water.

To serve: If you wish, add sour cream, fresh cream, or butter to the soup before serving. Croutons sautéed in butter make a good garnish. A nice touch to add, just before serving, is a *chiffonade* (finely cut strips) of dark-green lettuce leaves that have been blanched in boiling water for one minute.

PUREE OF CARROT SOUP

In France this soup is called *potage Crécy*—a word which used to evoke to me the fourteenth century battle in which Edward the Third defeated Phillipe de Valois, but after a long enough stay in France *Crécy* came to mean merely carrots or carrot soup. So much for history; in any case, the soup is well worth cooking.

INGREDIENTS FOR SEVEN TO NINE
DEPENDING UPON DESIRED THICKNESS

8 to 10 cups homemade chicken stock

1 lb 4 ounces carrots

4 Tbsp sour cream

salt and white pepper

To make: Clean the carrots well and cook them in some of the stock until quite soft. More stock is used than in green pea soup because carrots take much longer to cook than peas and there is more evaporation of liquid.) Proceed as with fresh green pea soup (see p. 13).

Note: The traditional recipe for *potage Crécy* uses rice or potatoes as the thickening agent, but a blender alone produces a finer result. The heavy cream used in some versions tastes good, but is a little heavy for my taste.

CREAM OF WATERCRESS SOUP

Cream of watercress soup is very much a summer soup and is good served cold, garnished with a few fresh leaves of cress.

INGREDIENTS FOR SIX

6 cups homemade chicken stock

1 bunch watercress, stems removed

2 medium potatoes, peeled and sliced

1 Tbsp butter

3 Tbsp sour cream ·

salt and pepper

To make: Clean the watercress. Melt the butter in a deep, thick-bottomed pot and cook the watercress over very low heat until limp. Add the potatoes and chicken stock. Cook until soft. Add salt and pepper. Puree the mixture in a blender a few cups at a time, adding some of the sour cream to each batch. Blend at low speed just until pureed. Reheat gently, stir, and serve.

SAUCES

ALMOST EVERYONE is familiar with the French states-
man Talleyrand's famous remark about the English:
"They have one sauce and a hundred religions." For
their part, the English like to intimate that the French
have contrived and use so many sauces because they
are obliged to mask inferior ingredients. Both sides in
this bickering are wrong; the inference that the French
use sauces to mask inferior ingredients is far from true.
The French cuisine is based on first-class ingredients,
and I'll gamble that any top-notch French chef would
readily admit that fine cooking is at least 50 percent
a matter of the quality of ingredients available. In fact,

far from masking foods with sauces, the French, for the most part, do not use anything but the meat juice (*jus*) from a fine bird or roast of meat; they do not make gravy by adding flour and water to the fat in the pan. In general, a good chef counts on one tablespoon of *jus* per serving of roast chicken. If more is needed or demanded, it is made by mixing reduced fresh chicken stock with the pan juices.

BASIC SAUCE

I couldn't cook without this sauce, and I am convinced that if you make it once it will become a major item of your cooking repertoire. As you will note, it is not at all difficult to make, and, although the process takes a good deal of time from beginning to end, the sauce doesn't require constant watching. One of its desirable characteristics is that all the fat is removed; the sauce is then clarified, which assures its purity and helps prevent its spoiling. A frozen batch can last for months.

Why should one go to the trouble of making a basic sauce? For many reasons: By adding this sauce to a brown roux (flour and butter mixed together and cooked over fairly high heat until it browns) you produce a superior brown sauce (called for in many recipes) totally unlike the canned gravy, bouillon cubes, or other substitutes usually resorted to. With this sauce you can make an aspic so palatable that you will realize how astonishingly good an aspic can be. A few tablespoons of this sauce mixed with butter, lemon juice, and a dash of cayenne make a superb steak sauce. One tablespoon plus a little butter does wonders for green beans or brussels sprouts, and braised lettuce with a few tablespoons becomes a luxury dish. Try adding chopped truffles to a cup of it and serving it as a sauce for roast beef.

INGREDIENTS FOR TWO QUARTS

4 lb beef bones with meat, or beef shank and bones

2½ lb veal bones with meat, or veal shank (If you can, prevail upon your butcher to chop the bones into small pieces.)

3 Tbsp oil

2 medium onions, each studded with a clove

3 stalks celery (with some of the leaves), roughly chopped

3 medium carrots, peeled and roughly chopped

10 sprigs parsley (stems as well as leaves)

2 medium bay leaves

½ tsp leaf thyme

3 Tbsp tomato paste

salt (Do not use too much; the stock becomes much reduced and consequently the salt ratio increases.)

8 peppercorns

2 cups dry white wine

1 cup dry Madeira or imported Graves (The Graves —French white wine from the Bordeaux region— in no way resembles the Madeira, but it has an unobtrusive softness that adds a fine flavor to this sauce.)

3 egg whites and crushed egg shells

Note: You may, if you wish, add a piece of ham to the meat and bones used for this sauce; it is traditional, but it doesn't add anything I want. However, do as you please.

To make: Preheat the oven to 500°. Place all the meat and bones in a large pan, put it in the oven, leaving it there only until the meat and bones have browned. Meanwhile, put some oil in a very large pot and brown the onions, celery, and carrots, stirring frequently. (If you don't have a pot large enough, use more than one and distribute the ingredients equally.) When the meat is browned, add it to the vegetables with the bay leaves, thyme, salt, parsley, and peppercorns. Add water to cover and bring slowly to a boil. Just as the liquid starts to get active, turn down the heat and remove the froth and scum from the surface. Continue skimming until the liquid is relatively clear. Do not pay any attention to the fat on the surface of the liquid; it will be taken care of later. Turn to the lowest heat that will keep the liquid simmering with a barely perceptible movement. After this, check every thirty minutes or so to see if the liquid has reduced. If it has, add hot water. After four hours the contents of the pot will begin to take on the appearance of slosh, but don't be alarmed; this slosh becomes transformed into a limpid, amber liquid with a most delicious flavor. Cook for seven hours all together. It takes that long to extract the substance from the bones—the substance that provides the unctuousness of the finished sauce and the natural gelatin, for this sauce jells beautifully when it is chilled.

After the fifth hour add the tomato paste and, little by little, the two cups of white wine. Add no water after the fifth hour. After the seventh hour allow the mixture to cool, then strain it through a not-too-fine sieve. Chill the liquid overnight in the refrigerator. The next day remove every bit of fat, which will not be difficult as it will be solidified. It is essential to get *all* the fat off; otherwise you won't be able to clarify the stock.

[21]

To clarify the liquid, lightly beat three egg whites and add them to the stock along with the crushed egg shells. Bring the stock slowly to a boil, stirring constantly to prevent the egg whites from scorching. As the stock comes to a boil, you will notice the separation of the substances that cloud the stock from the clear liquid. Turn off the heat and allow the clarification process to continue for ten minutes. Then, with a fine skimmer, carefully remove and reject as much of the frothy substance as you can. I say carefully because the froth is fragile, and there is no point in breaking up into the clear liquid what you have been attempting to separate from it.

Now—and this is the last and most important step— strain the liquid through a linen kitchen towel which has been soaked in cold water and wrung out. This is a somewhat slow process but, again, you need not watch it constantly. Pour a ladle or two on the towel and allow it to slowly drip through. When the strained particles begin to clog the porousness of the towel, carefully take it off the receptacle into which the clear stock is dripping and rinse it thoroughly in very hot water. Wring it out again and recommence the straining process. When this is completed, add the Madeira or Graves wine, mix it thoroughly, and pour the now completed sauce into freezer-proof plastic cups or glasses. Cover them well with foil and put them in the freezer. They will keep for months.

SAUCE BÉCHAMEL

I have read that *béchamel* is a dull sauce—as penetrating a comment as noting that water has little flavor. Even though the French cuisine has many other basic

---

sauces, I can't imagine what it would be like without *sauce béchamel*. Not as a corollary, but just as a thought, try to imagine the Chinese cuisine without its ubiquitous cornstarch-based *béchamel*, for that is indeed what it is. If, in addition, you took away the equally ubiquitous soy sauce, the Chinese cuisine for all practical purposes would be out of business.

In any case, because *sauce béchamel* is used in so many dishes—especially with vegetables and as a base for the following *sauce Mornay*—it is advisable to learn how to make it, and it is easy. The only important thing to note is that it can be made with a variety of liquids: milk, veal stock, chicken stock, fish or shellfish bouillon, and even vegetable bouillon, depending on how it is to be used. Here is the basic recipe.

INGREDIENTS FOR TWO AND ONE-HALF CUPS

3 Tbsp butter

3 Tbsp flour

2 cups milk, which have been brought to the boil

salt and white pepper

1 pinch nutmeg

To make: In a heavy-bottomed pot, melt the butter, add the flour, and, stirring constantly, cook and blend the two ingredients for a few minutes, but without browning them. Add a little of the hot milk and with a whisk blend until smooth. Add more milk, continue whisking, raise the heat, continue whisking, and cook until thoroughly blended. At this point, add the salt, pepper, and nutmeg. Ideally, this sauce should cook— but barely—for twenty minutes, preferably in a *bain-marie* or water bath.

[2 3]

SAUCE MORNAY

The French write about *sauce Mornay* more than they use it, but amateur American cooks seem to be devoted to it—probably because it has the faculty of masking just about all other flavors, which under certain circumstances is desirable. When it is well made and used appropriately, as with *oeufs Florentine, sauce Mornay* can be admirable.

To make: Make a *sauce béchamel* (see p. 22). Just before serving the dish your *sauce Mornay* is to accompany, add to the basic béchamel recipe one-fourth cup of roughly grated Swiss Gruyère cheese and one-fourth cup of very finely grated Parmesan. Mix thoroughly and serve immediately; if kept too long over heat, the cheese can become stringy and separate from the sauce, and, worse, the butter in the sauce can clarify and rise to the surface—an unappetizing sight.

SAUCE BÉARNAISE

I remember an American couple eating lunch next to me on the rue du Faubourg St. Honoré in Paris, staring as I spread *sauce Béarnaise* on my steak. I could sense that both of them—but especially the man—were having a terrible struggle and finally the man, secure in his confidence that I wouldn't understand what he was saying, said to his wife, "Look at that! He's eating steak with mayonnaise." I wasn't nettled. The American meat they were familiar with contains far too much fat to need a sauce as rich as *Béarnaise*. I dont serve it with steak, but I do with grilled fish and with poached eggs in a tartlet of puff paste, which I coat with the sauce and crown with a slice of poached marrow. It's too good to give up.

INGREDIENTS FOR ONE CUP

3 egg yolks

1 Tbsp dried tarragon

1 heaping Tbsp shallots, finely chopped (Use scallions if you cannot find shallots, but use a little more and only the white parts.)

¼ cup white wine vinegar

¼ cup dry white wine

1 piece bay leaf, the size of one-half a dime

a few leaves thyme

salt and white pepper

5 ounces butter, cut in pieces

a few drops lemon juice

$\frac{1}{10}$ tsp cayenne pepper

fresh tarragon (or parsley or chervil)

To make: Cook the shallots, tarragon, white wine, vinegar, salt, pepper, bay leaf, and thyme over high heat until only one-third of the original mixture remains. Allow to cool somewhat. Add the egg yolks mixed with a teaspoon of water, and over low heat (or use a double boiler, but don't let the water in the bottom section boil), whisking or stirring with a wooden spoon, cook until the yolks begin to thicken—about eighteen minutes. Don't hurry this phase; just when you think nothing is happening, there it is. Then add the butter in four batches, whisking or stirring constantly. When all the

[25]

butter has been added and the sauce is smooth, put it through a sieve and keep warm in a heated water bath. If you have a little fresh tarragon, chop it up and add it to the sauce after it has been strained; if not, add a little chopped parsley or chervil to brighten up the appearance of the sauce. Add the cayenne pepper and lemon juice to taste.

MAYONNAISE

To put it plainly, homemade mayonnaise is not even related to the bottled commercial products sold under the same name. True mayonnaise is a not-too-stable miracle of unctuousness, best when made and served for the moment, and its flavor is totally unlike anything else —least of all, the bottled variety. I have nothing against the commercial products; they have their uses. For instance, a club sandwich made with sliced breast of chicken (not turkey), crisp bacon, slices of tomato, and tender lettuce is an inspired combination, but it needs some sort of dressing. True mayonnaise will not do; it is too heavy for a sandwich. A boiled dressing or one of the non-sweet commercial dressings is required. Dyed-in-the-wool mayonnaise comes into the picture with cold lobster, shrimp, or crab meat—essentially dry foods. Its relatives *Aioli* (mayonnaise with garlic) and *rouille* (mayonnaise with Spanish paprika) are staples of the Mediterranean world, where they point up everything from boiled potatoes to grilled lobster. Certain foods seem eminently reasonable in different parts of the world. In the Mediterranean area olive oil and garlic are nothing more than sensible items of everyone's diet. (They wouldn't be bad for us, for that matter.)

One important rule in making mayonnaise is that the eggs and the oil should be at room temperature. Although it is possible to make mayonnaise with one egg yolk, it is not usually practicable, unless you have a small, high-sided mortar with a pestle or a whisk that just fits a bowl. There is no mystery to why this should be so; an ordinary bowl in which one uses a hand or electric beater does not provide enough contact between one egg yolk and the blades of the beater to assure the emulsification of the yolk and the oil. With two egg yolks it is much easier, and you have more mayonnaise, which will keep for a day or so in the refrigerator.

INGREDIENTS FOR ONE AND ONE-HALF CUPS

2 egg yolks

salt and white pepper

olive oil

juice of ½ lemon, strained

1 Tbsp boiling water

½ tsp Dijon mustard or ¼ tsp dried mustard (optional)

To make: Put the egg yolks into a bowl with the salt, pepper, and mustard (if you decide to use it). Whisk or beat this mixture for a few minutes until it is thoroughly blended; then begin adding oil, a little at a time. If you use an electric beater you need not interrupt the beating; add the oil with one hand while the other controls the beater. This is the crucial moment. If the oil emulsifies with the egg yolks, you are in business, but be careful to add only a little oil at a time until you have accumulated a substantial amount of the emulsified mixture, from which point you may add oil in larger quantities, continuing until the mixture is firm enough to maintain its shape when spooned on a plate. Now add the lemon juice and mix well while adding olive oil to produce the thickness you prefer. Add the boiling water and mix it in very quickly with a spoon. If after adding, say, one-half cup oil, the oil remains separated from the yolks, you can assume that it is not going to emulsify. However, this does not mean that all is lost. Put another egg yolk into a clean bowl, beat or whisk it for a minute or so, and begin adding the mixture that did not emulsify. (Another method of rectifying non-emulsified mayonnaise is to mix one teaspoon mustard with one tablespoon of the non-emulsified mixture and proceed as above, but, although it does not give you too much mayonnaise, it does give you too much mustard to my taste.)

GASCON BUTTER

The term *butter* in Gascon butter is sardonic; there is very little butter in Périgord. This recipe is for those who like garlic, but sometimes find the flavor a bit acrid. To tell the truth, I also find that garlic is a bit more acrid than it should be; it is a matter of how fresh it is for one thing and, for another, where is was grown. The garlic of the French Midi, for example, is always digestible and perhaps because everyone eats it, there is never any question of odor.

This is a Périgourdine recipe, which means that goose, ham, or pork fat would be substituted for butter, but any oil or fat with a good flavor will do. I prefer olive oil.

INGREDIENTS

4 large cloves garlic, peeled

2 Tbsp olive oil, butter, or whatever oil you wish

salt and pepper

To make: Throw the garlic cloves into a little boiling water. Turn down the heat and simmer for fifteen minutes. Drain the cloves of garlic, put them into a mortar or bowl, add the other ingredients, and pound or mash thoroughly until the mixture is smooth.

To use: Try Gascon butter on grilled mushrooms, or mix it into white or red beans to be served as a garnish for a roast leg of lamb or a poached ham. Gascon butter can also be used to make a genteel version of garlic bread or to complement sauces that need a mild lift.

VINAIGRETTE SAUCE

Vinaigrette sauce is probably the most-used sauce in the French cuisine—it figures in most hors d'oeuvre and salads and it is also served with some vegetables, for example, a whole artichoke. The usual ratio of oil to vinegar is three to one, but this may be varied to suit certain foods. A bean salad, being bland, requires more vinegar and a delicate lettuce salad is best with a vinaigrette with less vinegar. In almost every case, fresh lemon juice can be substituted for vinegar.

I prefer olive oil in vinaigrette, but peanut oil is very good and many people prefer its more neutral flavor. Incidently, peanut oil does not taste of peanuts—it has virtually no flavor at all.

A little hot mustard (Dijon) may be mixed into vinaigrette; but be very careful, it can be overpowering. One-eighth teaspoon for six tablespoons of olive oil and two tablespoons of vinegar would be about right.

Another sauce, related to the vinaigrettte, is a simple mixture of melted butter and lemon juice. This is perfect for tepid or hot asparagus and artichokes. It would be out of the question with salad greens of any kind.

HOLLANDAISE SAUCE

Hollandaise sauce is a classic and belongs in every cook's repertoire. It presents no particular difficulty except that, like *crème anglaise* and *sauce Béarnaise*, it demands patience.

INGREDIENTS FOR TWO CUPS
OR EIGHT SERVINGS

4 egg yolks

7 ounces melted butter

2 or more Tbsp lemon juice

salt and white pepper

[3 0]

To make: Beat the egg yolks until smooth but not over-aerated. Rinse out the top of a double boiler with cold water; the bottom section should contain warm, but not hot, water. Put the egg yolks in the top section of the double boiler, turn up the heat somewhat, and, with a whisk or an ordinary egg beater, begin stirring the egg yolks. (A whisk is best for beating because it contacts every part of the interior of the pot.) As with all sauces involving the cooking of egg yolks, the crucial moment occurs when you have almost become convinced that nothing is going to happen. Don't falter at this point; just carry on, and the egg yolks will turn creamy. When this happens, add the lemon juice and salt and pepper and continue whisking or beating. If the mixture seems to be thickening too rapidly—keep a close eye on the bottom of the pot for signs of this— lift the top part of the double boiler from the hot water and stir very rapidly. When the situation is under control again, return the mixture to the hot water and continue as before. When the yolk mixture is thick enough to coat the whisk and the sides of the pot, re- move the top of the double boiler from the hot water and start adding the melted butter, a bit at a time, whisking continuously. Continue whisking until all the butter has been incorporated. Hollandaise sauce should be served tepid.

ORANGE SAUCE

Orange sauce is not as exotic in flavor as you might imagine, and it is a nice change. As you will note, it is a variation of hollandaise sauce.

[31]

INGREDIENTS FOR TWO CUPS
OR EIGHT SERVINGS

hollandaise sauce (see p. 30)

*the zest (the thin, orange-colored, outside skin
of the fruit) of 1 orange*

orange juice to taste

½ tsp lemon juice

To make: Proceed precisely as for hollandaise sauce,
but add the zest of the orange to the yolks before beating them. The juices listed above replace the lemon
juice in the hollandaise recipe and are added (as in
hollandaise) when the egg yolks become creamy.

HORS
D'OEUVRE

AN HORS D'OEUVRE in France can mean anything from
a cucumber salad (cucumbers salted, drained, and
dressed with oil, vinegar, and very finely chopped parsley) to a flamboyant spread such as I once encountered
in a famous Provençal restaurant. The *hors d'oeuvre*
consisted of sixty-five different items and was appropriately called "an avalanche of *hors d'oeuvre* of the
1900 period." After tackling the avalanche, which was

excellent, we weren't interested in much else—and there were a good many other courses we just didn't get to. Personally, I like the idea of the cucumber salad, and there are many other similar salads: tomato, *céleri rémoulade*, marinated roast peppers, artichoke hearts, and so forth. Tasting and savoring one well-seasoned, fine fresh vegetable is truly an appetite opener or appetizer, our term for the French *hors d'oeuvre*. My complaint about our appetizers is that they tend to be hackneyed: shrimp cocktail, melon, clams, pâté—all very nice, but usually nondescript and eventually boring. I think that Americans in particular, given the amount of meat we eat, should attempt to present a vegetable *hors d'oeuvre* as a balance. Vegetables, of course, have the added advantage of being notably low in cholesterol and fats.

AN ASSORTMENT OF HARD-BOILED EGG DISHES

Everyone has tasted picnic-type stuffed or deviled eggs made with bottled mayonnaise, but there are more interesting preparations of hard-boiled eggs, some of which are not stuffed but rather sliced and masked with various purees and sauces. Try a variety of the following dishes as part of a summer buffet lunch.

Note: All the following recipes call for mayonnaise or for sour cream dressing. The mayonnaise is the homemade variety—an emulsion of egg yolks, olive oil, lemon juice (or good vinegar), salt, pepper, and sometimes a little Dijon or dried English mustard. The basic recipe for mayonnaise is on p. 26. To make sour cream dressing, mix one cup sour cream with one tablespoon lemon juice (or wine vinegar), salt, pepper, and, if you wish, one-half teaspoon Dijon mustard or a pinch of dried, hot mustard. It doesn't hurt, although it isn't necessary, to add two tablespoons olive oil.

OEUFS À LA CRESSONNIÈRE FOR EIGHT

8 eggs, hard-boiled

1¼ cups mayonnaise with lemon

½ tsp Dijon mustard

watercress

1561142

To make: Puree enough watercress leaves (reject the stems) to color the mayonnaise—about one-fourth cup of puree. Mix it into the mayonnaise with the mustard. Place the halved hard-boiled eggs on a platter, cut-side down. Coat the eggs with the watercress-mayonnaise mixture.

To serve: Decorate with a few sprigs of watercress, the leaves with part of the stems.

EGGS WITH SHRIMP FOR EIGHT

8 eggs, hard-boiled

1 lb cooked shrimp (one-half to be pureed and mixed into the mayonnaise, one-half to be used as a garnish)

1 cup mayonnaise

1 Tbsp olive oil

1 Tbsp lemon juice

⅛ tsp cayenne pepper

To make: Puree one-half pound of the shrimps in a blender with the olive oil, lemon juice, and cayenne pepper. If necessary for blending purposes, use a little more oil. Mix this puree into the mayonnaise. Slice the eggs thin and place the slices in overlapping circles on a platter. Spread the mayonnaise-shrimp mixture over the egg slices. (If you wish, use one cup of sour cream instead of the mayonnaise. Mix in dried dillweed or chopped fresh dill. Otherwise proceed exactly as with the mayonnaise.)

To serve: Garnish the edges of the platter with the other one-half pound of shrimp and a few sprigs of parsley.

EGGS WITH TUNA FOR EIGHT

8 eggs, hard-boiled

canned tuna fish, the imported kind packed in olive oil (The quantity should be equal to the quantity of the 8 egg yolks. Do not drain the tuna; the oil is delicious.)

2 Tbsp lemon juice

⅛ tsp cayenne pepper

1 cup mayonnaise

2 Tbsp tomato paste

8 small shrimp, or 8 black olives (optional)

To make: Halve the eggs and carefully remove the yolks. Set the whites aside. Mash the yolks with an equal quantity of undrained tuna. Season this mixture with lemon juice and cayenne pepper and fill the whites of the eggs, heaping the mixture without smoothing the surface. Mix the tomato paste into the mayonnaise and spread it on a serving dish. Place the stuffed egg halves on it, distributing them attractively.

[3 6]

To serve: Garnish each half with a small shrimp or a black olive.

EGGS WITH ANCHOVY PASTE FOR EIGHT

8 eggs, hard-boiled

1¼ cups mayonnaise with lemon juice

2 Tbsp anchovy paste, or to taste

5 black olives, chopped

parsley sprigs

To make: Halve the eggs and place cut-side down on a platter. Mask them with the mayonnaise flavored with the anchovy paste.

To serve: Garnish the platter by sprinkling the chopped black olives in a slender ring around the platter. Add a few sprigs of parsley.

EGGS WITH TOMATOES AND TUNA FOR EIGHT

8 hard-boiled eggs, whites and yolks chopped together

3 medium tomatoes, peeled, seeded, and chopped

2 small cans imported tuna packed in olive oil, undrained

olive oil

lemon juice

⅛ tsp cayenne pepper

black olives

[37]

To make: Mix the chopped tomatoes with the chopped eggs. In a blender or a mortar, make a puree of tuna. Add just enough olive oil and lemon juice to make a smooth puree. Season with cayenne pepper. Put the egg and tomato mixture into a shallow bowl and cover with the puree of tuna.

To serve: Decorate with whole or sliced black olives.

EGGS WITH CURRY FOR EIGHT

8 hard-boiled eggs, chopped

1¼ cups mayonnaise with lemon juice and 1 tsp curry powder

1 large, firm apple, peeled and chopped

To make: Mix the chopped eggs with the chopped apple. Do not let the mixture stand or the apples will become discolored. Cover with the curry mayonnaise and serve immediately.

EGGS WITH MUSHROOMS FOR EIGHT

¼ lb very fresh mushrooms, peeled

8 eggs, hard-boiled

salt and pepper

1 Tbsp lemon juice

chives, very finely chopped, or onions, grated

parsley sprigs

To make: Puree the mushrooms (uncooked) in a blender. Carefully separate the egg yolks from the whites, and set the whites aside. Combine the puree and the egg yolks, and add the lemon juice, salt, and pepper. Fill the whites, heaping the mixture.

To serve: Sprinkle with very finely chopped chives, or, if you wish, add a little grated onion to the mixture. Decorate with sprigs of parsley.

EGGS WITH CAVIAR FOR EIGHT

2 ounces pressed caviar (preferably fresh)

8 eggs, hard-boiled

2 Tbsp sour cream

1 Tbsp lemon juice

parsley sprigs

To make: Carefully separate the egg yolks from the whites. Set the whites aside. Mash the caviar with the yolks, sour cream, and lemon juice. Fill the whites, heaping the mixture into mounds.

To serve: Decorate with sprigs of parsley.

ANCHOIADE

Anchoiade, probably the most characteristic of Provençal dishes, is undoubtedly one of the oldest European recipes—it is a good deal over two thousand years old—to have come down to us unchanged in any way. If you try it, perhaps you will understand why it has endured, although I will admit that a taste for anchovies must be acquired—a process that usually takes just long enough for the aroma of a well-made *anchoiade* to reach one's nostrils. The best anchovies for this dish are the sort sold in bulk in Italian, Greek, and Spanish markets, but they must be desalted, skinned, and boned, which takes only a few seconds (see p. 270). A more convenient product is good-quality anchovy paste. If neither is avialable, use the ubiquitous canned fillets, but drain them well; the oil is too salty.

INGREDIENTS FOR SIX
WHEN SERVED AS AN APPETIZER

1 long loaf French or Italian bread

¾ cup olive oil

4 Tbsp well-mashed anchovies or the same quantity of anchovy paste

2 cloves garlic, very finely mashed

3 tsp red wine vinegar

pepper

To make: Mix all the ingredients, except the bread, until they are smoothly blended. Cut the loaf of bread in half lengthwise. Slash each half-loaf crosswise into fairly narrow slices, but do not cut all the way through. (This makes the *anchoiade* easier to handle; when cooked, the slices can be easily cut through with a sharp knife.) Spread the mixture over the bread, as evenly as possible, pressing the bits of garlic into the soft interior of the bread with a stale crust of bread. Put the *anchoiade* in a preheated 400° oven and bake until brown and crisp.

In a variation of *anchoiade*, I use chives instead of garlic, then add fresh or dried tarragon and pitted black olives, which have been soaked in cold water for fifteen minutes and drained. One tablespoon of chopped, fresh tarragon or one teaspoon of dried leaf tarragon will suffice; three-fourths cup of black olives will do. Don't hesitate to bash the olives up in the sauce; *anchoiade* does not depend on appearance for appeal—it doesn't need it.

Note: I wouldn't whisper this suggestion in Provence, but if you can't abide oil, substitute melted butter or a mixture of butter and oil. It goes without saying, I hope, that here as elsewhere only the very best olive oil should be used.

PUREE OF ITALIAN GREEN PEPPERS

You may be familiar with *caviar d'aubergines*, a puree of eggplant, oil, lemon, and garlic (see p. 45). This puree of grilled Italian green peppers is in the same category, but I think the peppers are more interesting; their flavor goes very well with drinks.

INGREDIENTS FOR SIX
WHEN SERVED AS AN APPETIZER

1 lb Italian green peppers (Italian peppers are long, sharply pointed, and light green. They are not hot. Cut them in half lengthwise. Remove and reject the stems, seeds, and membranes.)

olive oil (to coat the peppers before grilling and to mix into them after they are cooked)

juice of ½ lemon

salt and pepper

To make: Put the halved peppers, skin-side up, on a piece of doubled aluminum foil. Brush each half with olive oil and put them under the broiler or—and I do prefer it—in a very hot oven. Keep the peppers under the broiler or in the oven only until the skin can be removed easily. This isn't hard to determine; the skin wrinkles when it has separated from the pulp. When they seem done, take the peppers out of the oven or from under the grill and set them aside to cool. When they are cool, peel off the skins, but be careful not to lose any of the pepper juice, which contains a good deal of the flavor. Put the peppers and juice in a bowl, then add two tablespoons of olive oil and the lemon juice. Mash with a fork until the mixture resembles a puree. Add salt and pepper and continue mashing and stirring. The puree can be kept in the refrigerator for several days, but it must be mixed very well after standing for any length of time; the oil naturally rises to the surface.

PORK SHANKS IN WINE ASPIC

Although I had known of it for years (and, to tell the truth, somewhat disdained it), I first tasted pork shanks in wine aspic for lunch at the restaurant Larue in Paris a few years before its regrettable closing in 1954. I recall my surprise at encountering what I regarded as a middle-European specialty in one of the proudest bastions of *la haute cuisine française*, and remember wondering how it got there. In due time I learned that in 1908 Eduard Nignon and his chef, Celestin Duplat, had come directly from l'Hermitage in Leningrad—where their success had been great—to Larue on the rue Royale —where, if anything, their success was even more brilliant. What could be more natural than that certain

Russian specialties should be incorporated into the menu—especially since the grand dukes and the other wealthy Russians they had served were as often in Paris as they were in Moscow, Leningrad, or Baden-Baden. One of these Russian dishes, *Koulibiak* (a mixture of poached salmon, *kasha*, *vesiga* [sturgeon marrow], hard-boiled eggs, and a good deal of butter—all encased in brioche pastry), is still a specialty of Le Pavillon in New York.

Regardless of its origin, pork shanks in wine aspic is delectable, especially when served as part of an *hors d'oeuvre varié* as it was at Larue. Surprisingly enough, it is not at all difficult to make, but it does take time—its preparation, that is—and must be made well in advance.

INGREDIENTS FOR SIX TO EIGHT

3½ lb pork shanks

1 large onion, studded with 2 cloves

1 large bay leaf

¼ tsp thyme

1 handful parsley (stems as well as leaves)

2 medium carrots, scraped and roughly chopped

2 stalks celery (leaves included), roughly chopped

½ tsp hot red pepper (not cayenne, but the sort Italians use)

salt and pepper

1 envelope unflavored gelatine

1 cup white wine (preferably Graves, imported from France, but any other good-quality, not-too-dry or not-too-sweet white wine will do).

parsley, very, very finely chopped (optional)

To make: Put the pork shanks in a large pot, cover well with cold water, and bring slowly to a boil. When the water begins to boil, turn down the heat and skim off any froth or scum. Leave the heat as low as it will go and, except for skimming from time to time, forget the shanks for two hours. Then add the onion, bay leaf, thyme, handful of parsley, carrots, celery, hot red pepper, salt, and pepper and continue to cook the mixture at a simmer for two more hours. At this point test with a fork to see if the bones are loosening from the meat. If they are not, continue cooking until they do. Then carefully lift out the pork shanks and remove and reject the bones. Put the shanks (or pieces of shanks— don't worry about how they look) in a glass, china, or glazed earthenware bowl. Strain the liquid, reject the strained vegetables, and pour just enough of the liquid over the meat to cover it. Allow it to cool somewhat, then put the dish in the refrigerator overnight or until the fat congeals on the surface and the liquid firms into aspic.

The final and most important step follows. Remove all the fat from the surface of the jelled stock. Melt the jelled stock (which contains the meat) over low heat just to the point at which the meat can be removed with a perforated spoon. Remove the meat and put it into the dish from which you intend to serve it (it should be glass, china, or glazed earthenware). Bring the stock to a boil, strain it through a fine sieve, and add to it the gelatine dissolved in a small amount of white wine. (The commercial gelatine is added because wine, or any other alcohol, inhibits jellification.) When the stock has cooled somewhat, add one cup of good quality white wine. Pour the liquid over the meat. Chill the mixture of meat and liquid until it becomes firm. If you like, sprinkle very, very finely chopped parsley over the surface of the aspic.

To serve: Offer the pork shanks in wine aspic as part of an *hors d'oeuvre varié* or as a first course for lunch with *pommes à l'huile.* Rye bread goes particularly well with this dish, as does genuinely crusty French bread. Regardless of when served, it should be accompanied by a vinaigrette sauce with chopped shallots or scallions, served from a sauce-boat.

CAVIAR D'AUBERGINES

The name *caviar d'aubergines* is not so much ostentatious as sardonic. One of the best of the many ways in which eggplant can be prepared, this dish is most useful as an hors d'oeuvre or as part of a buffet.

INGREDIENTS FOR FIFTEEN
WHEN SERVED AS AN HORS D'OEUVRE

2 medium eggplants

juice of 1 medium lemon or lime

4 cloves garlic (If you have inhibitions about garlic, substitute very finely chopped chives, scallions, or grated onion.)

4 Tbsp parsley, very finely chopped

olive oil, as desired

salt and freshly ground black pepper

To make: Put the whole, washed but untrimmed, eggplants on a doubled piece of aluminum foil and place under the broiler, set at 375°. Since the flesh is firmest toward the stem end, cook the eggplants until that end is soft, turning from time to time. Do not be disturbed if the large end seems overcooked or takes on the appearance of a deflated balloon; as long as the skin is intact, the meaty, inside part cannot burn.

When done, put the eggplants on a dish and set them aside to cool. When cool enough to handle, hold each eggplant by the stem end over a plate, slit with a knife, and remove the flesh with a wooden, silver, or stainless steel spoon, taking care not to lose any of the juice. Then, with a silver or stainless steel fork, begin mashing the eggplant pulp. Add the oil, starting with from two to four tablespoons, and continue mashing. The amount of oil is optional, but I prefer to hold it down. Then add the lemon or lime juice, parsley, garlic (which has been put through a squeezer), salt, and pepper. Mash and mix until very smooth.

Caviar d'aubergines may be made well in advance, but must be covered and sealed with clear plastic wrap to prevent oxidation, and chilled. Mix again just before serving. Very finely chopped, peeled, seeded, and drained tomatoes in the quantity of one medium tomato to each eggplant may be added to the mixture.

RAW MUSHROOM SALAD

Nothing brings out the subtle flavor of mushrooms quite so well as raw mushroom salad, a simple but delicate preparation. It can be made only with very fresh mushrooms—that is, mushrooms that have not opened to form the only too familiar and not very appetizing black-lined umbrella effect. Believe it or not, mushrooms can be had fresh almost everywhere, although they are not always visible. The explanation for this is that—rather like those people who, in order to avoid wasting one-half a loaf of bread, eat stale bread all their lives—the produce people leave a basket of mushrooms out until it is sold, which, given the prices, sometimes takes quite a while. In the meantime, the fresh mushrooms in the back of the store are also maturing so that, when brought out, they too become overripe very quickly. If, in the middle of this uncalculated, but nevertheless devastating, campaign of mushroom detrition, you manage to find some really fresh mushrooms, try this recipe.

INGREDIENTS FOR SIX

1 lb mushrooms

juice of 1 medium lemon

3 Tbsp olive oil

salt and pepper

To make: If the mushrooms are very fresh, they will not need washing; merely wipe them with a damp cloth. Peel the mushrooms and trim off part of the stems if they are long, just the ends if they are short. (To peel mushrooms quickly takes practice, but even more important is a small, very sharp knife. Hold the knife in one hand—it does not move—and turn the mushroom against the blade with your other hand. If you are so inclined, save the peelings and use them to flavor a sauce.) Slice the peeled mushrooms and marinate them in lemon juice, olive oil, salt, and pepper for two hours in the refrigerator.

To serve: Serve as is or with a very light sprinkling of finely chopped parsley. Actually this hors d'oeuvre is best as part of a light, but varied, first course of cold dishes: for example, a bit of pâté, some sliced tomatoes with basil and oil, hard-boiled eggs with mayonnaise, and sardines with butter.

POACHED EGGS FLORENTINE

The names of some French dishes denote an ingredient or garnish which may turn up in a number of recipes. For example, *Mirabeau* means anchovy fillets, black olives, and blanched tarragon leaves; *Mornay* means a much overused cheese sauce; *Rossini* means truffles and *foie gras; parmentière* means potatoes; and *Florentine* means spinach. Other names have caused nothing but trouble; for example, *homard à l'américaine* (lobster American) has produced a whole mess of rather stupid explanations by French writers of how the dish could possibly have acquired such a name. In their chauvinism, none seems to have noted that no one in America has ever claimed *homard à l'américaine* although it is excellent. *Sauce allemande* (German sauce) is a denomination that proves intermittently embarrassing, although French writers hasten to point out that it, *crème anglaise,* and *sauce espagnole* are strictly French sauces, which they are, but there is no need to get excited about the matter.

Eggs Florentine are superb as a luncheon dish, but they can also figure very well as part of a not-too-large buffet. They should be served hot.

INGREDIENTS FOR FOUR TO SIX

2 packages frozen chopped spinach

8 eggs, poached (see p. 85)

2 cups sauce Mornay (see p. 24)

1 Tbsp Parmesan cheese, finely grated

3 ounces butter

salt and pepper

To make: Cook the spinach in one-half cup lightly salted water. After the spinach is thoroughly thawed, cook it for no more than three or four minutes, stirring constantly. Then put it in an oven set at 200°. Make the *sauce Mornay* and keep it warm in a water bath. Poach the eggs and keep them in water just warm enough to keep the chill off. Quickly drain the spinach, mix in two ounces of the butter, the salt and pepper, and spread the spinach on a heated platter. Drain the eggs and place them on the spinach in an attractive pattern, cover the whole with the *Mornay,* and sprinkle with the grated Parmesan cheese and the other ounce of butter (which has been melted). Put the dish under the broiler for a matter of seconds, or just long enough to produce a slight brownish glaze on the surface. Serve immediately.

The above is the classical recipe, but there are other equally attractive versions. For example:

Add garlic and a good pinch of nutmeg to the spinach and, in addition to the grated cheese, add a very fine dusting of bread crumbs.

Mix the spinach with sour cream, garlic, and nutmeg. Coat the dish lightly with *sauce Mornay* and put under the broiler.

Mix the spinach with *sauce béchamel* (see p. 22), coat with *sauce Mornay,* and continue as above.

POACHED EGGS WITH ARTICHOKE HEARTS AND TARRAGON SAUCE

The notable feature of this recipe—aside from the fact that it tastes very good—is the absence of butter in the sauce. Try it, and you will see that it simply doesn't need it.

INGREDIENTS FOR FOUR

4 artichoke hearts

4 eggs, poached (see p. 85)

1¼ cups beef stock

1½ tsp all-purpose flour

1 Tbsp dried tarragon

2 egg yolks

pinch of cayenne pepper

juice of ¼ lemon

salt (very little, as the stock is usually salty)

To make: Prepare artichoke hearts as directed on p. 202 or use imported French canned artichoke hearts. (If you use the canned variety, wash them well in cold water. Heat them and keep warm in water to which a little lemon juice has been added.) Add the tarragon to the beef stock and simmer for fifteen minutes. In another pot mix the flour with enough water to make a smooth blend. Strain the beef stock into the flour-water mixture, stirring to amalgamate the flour and stock. Cook for five minutes, stirring constantly. Take the pot off the heat and add two egg yolks, lightly beaten with a little cold water; pour them into the beef stock-flour mixture a little at a time while stirring constantly. Cook the mixture over low heat, stirring constantly, until the sauce coats the spoon. Add the cayenne pepper, salt, and lemon juice, and mix thoroughly. Keep the sauce warm by putting the pot in a larger pot or a saucepan of warm water (this makes an improvised *bain-marie*). Poach four eggs. Place the artichoke hearts on a small platter, put an egg on each one, and strain the sauce over all.

To serve: If you have some fresh tarragon at hand, sprinkle one teaspoon, chopped, on the eggs or sprinkle the whole with one tablespoon of very, very finely chopped parsley.

Note: Don't be put off by the stirring and straining; it doesn't take that much time to make this dish, and the result is worth it.

COLD POACHED EGGS ALICE B. TOKLAS

I first made cold poached eggs Alice B. Toklas in the south of France where, with virtually no help from creative cooks, the superb vegetables, herbs, and incomparable olive oil of the region seem to compose themselves into marvelously appetizing combinations. However, Alice Toklas had a good deal to do with the development of this dish. As she frequently said, she

liked *corsé* food (*corsé* translates as *forthright*), especially garlic, and once having tasted this Provençal as-
semblage which I put together with bits of the environ-
ment, she insisted on having it as often as possible.
Since she considered it a light sort of appetizer, I sometimes made it for our lunch day after day. She firmly
believed that this sort of food was good for everyone,
and, as she lived to be only a few months short of what
were ninety remarkably full years and was lucid to the
last, I dare say there is something to her belief.

INGREDIENTS FOR SIX

3 very large, dead-ripe, unblemished tomatoes

6 eggs, poached or coddled (see p. 85)

FOR THE SAUCE

*large handful of fresh basil leaves or 1 Tbsp dried
basil (Fresh basil is infinitely preferable to dried
basil, but it is better to resort to the dried variety
than to forego the dish.)*

*3 cloves garlic, peeled and put through a garlic
press*

½ to ⅔ cup olive oil

juice of ½ lemon

½ tsp Dijon mustard or a pinch of dried mustard

2 Tbsp chives, chopped

salt and pepper

6 anchovies (optional)

6 capers (optional)

Note: If you don't like garlic, if it doesn't like you,
or if you are uncertain about your guests' preferences

on this matter, omit it or reduce the quantity. The dish won't be the same, however.

To make: Drop the tomatoes into boiling water for fifteen seconds, remove them, and put them into cold water; the skins can then be easily removed. Do not put more than one tomato at a time into the boiling water or the temperature of the water will be lowered to the point that, beyond washing the tomatoes, nothing will happen. Peel the tomatoes, cut off and reject the blossom and stem ends, and cut the tomatoes in half. This will give you six thick slices, one for each egg. If you use coddled eggs, make a little hollow in each tomato slice to prevent the eggs from rolling off; poached eggs will stay put.

To make the sauce, chop the basil leaves into fine strips and put them into a deep bowl. Add all ingredients except the anchovies and capers, and with a pestle or heavy spoon mash until the mixture is smooth.

To serve: Put a slice of tomato on each plate. Place an egg on each slice and pour sauce over the egg and tomato. If you like anchovies, put a rolled anchovy with a caper on each egg.

KIDNEY BEANS WITH POACHED EGGS, TOMATOES, AND MAYONNAISE

If this combination startles you, so much the better. You will be surprised, I think, by what turns out to be an ethereal blend of flavors and textures with each ingredient somehow enhanced. The kidney beans, more accustomed to oil, vinegar, and garlic than the gentle and elegant company of mayonnaise, seem to become

[5 3]

more flavorful, the poached eggs more unctuous, and the tomato just tart enough to get all that blandness off the ground. Curiously, and despite the beans, this is an understated dish that people invariably recognize as good food. When I have served it, I have never had to wonder what to do with leftovers.

INGREDIENTS FOR EIGHT

2 lb canned red kidney beans

1½ cups mayonnaise with a slight exaggeration of lemon juice (see p. 26)

8 large eggs, poached (see p. 85)

4 medium tomatoes, peeled, seeded, and roughly chopped

2 Tbsp parsley, very finely chopped

salt and pepper

paprika (optional)

To make: Drain the beans, but not too thoroughly, and reject the drained liquid. Put the beans in a shallow bowl, mix in the mayonnaise, the tomatoes, and the parsley. Add as much salt and pepper as suits you and, if necessary, more lemon juice. Place the poached eggs on the beans, disposing them as attractively as possible. That's all there is to it. However, if you find the poached eggs thus displayed too nude, make a little more mayonnaise, coat each egg with a bit of it, and sprinkle with paprika.

To serve: This dish, which makes a fine first course for a lunch served outdoors in a garden or on a terrace, absolutely demands the accompaniment of French bread and red wine.

GUACAMOLE

Guacamole is quite flexible; it can be served in halved avocado shells, in mounds on lettuce, or in stuffed tomatoes as filling. I like it best as a cocktail, buffet, or pre-dinner appetizer to accompany drinks—served on thinly sliced white bread which has been dried in the oven. *Guacamole* is also good as a dip, but I am not fond of dips—a personal prejudice. The following is enough for six individual servings or amply serves fifteen as part of a buffet or an *hors d'oeuvre varié.*

INGREDIENTS

3 medium, dead-ripe, unblemished avocados

1 cup mayonnaise, preferably homemade
(see page 26)

10 ounces (cleaned weight) cooked shrimp, finely
chopped

1 medium onion, peeled and grated

juice of 1 lime or small lemon

Tabasco sauce or cayenne pepper, to taste

1 medium tomato, skinned, seeded, and finely
chopped

To make: Halve the avocados and reject the pits. If you plan to serve stuffed avocados, remove the pulp carefully in order not to damage the skins. In any case, put the pulp in a bowl and add the mayonnaise, lime or lemon juice, grated onion, and Tabasco sauce. Mash with a silver or stainless steel fork until the mixture is smooth. Then fold in the shrimp and chopped tomato.

Because avocados quickly become discolored, it is best to make this just before serving. Since avocados are very bland, however, more lime or lemon juice than is indicated above may be used to keep them fresh colored; or you may mash the avocados with the lime or lemon juice and the grated onion, spread the surface well with the mayonnaise, and cover the dish with clear plastic wrap. In this way you can prepare the ingredients one hour in advance and assemble them just before serving.

If you wish to serve *guacamole* as a filling for six stuffed tomatoes, halve the above amounts and omit the chopped tomato. To prepare tomatoes for stuffing, slice off and reject the stem ends. With a spoon, remove and reject the seeds and pulp from the insides. Sprinkle the insides with salt, turn the tomatoes upside down on a plate, and set aside for twenty minutes. A good deal of the vegetable's water will drain onto the plate. Dry the insides with paper towels before stuffing.

To prepare oven-cooked toast: Slice firm-textured white bread very thin. Remove the crust. Put the slices on a baking sheet and into a 350° oven. Watch carefully, removing them one by one as they brown. The slices will curl somewhat, but that doesn't matter. Do not butter.

To serve: A nice garnish, regardless of how you use *guacamole,* is a light sprinkling of very finely chopped black olives.

[5 6]

CROQUE MONSIEUR

Contrary to my wife's belief that the dish should properly be called "croak monsieur," *croque monsieur* can
serve as a very tasty cocktail snack. The ingredients
are familiar, and (as you will no doubt deduce) the
idea itself is the forerunner of our only-too-familiar
grilled cheese sandwich. However, there is a little more
to it; ham is also involved, the cheese is Gruyère rather
than the substance known as American cheese, and the
sandwich is not grilled, but sautéed—or fried, if you will.

INGREDIENTS FOR ONE SANDWICH

*2 slices good-quality white bread, with crusts
removed*

1 slice ham

1 slice Gruyère or Emmenthal cheese

Dijon mustard

paprika or cayenne pepper

butter

To make: On one piece of bread place a slice of ham
that just fits the bread, add a slice of Gruyère or Emmenthal cheese a little smaller than the bread (cheese
has a tendency to run when it is cooked), a light coating of Dijon mustard, and a dusting of paprika (or, as
I prefer, a faint sprinkling of cayenne pepper). Cover
with another piece of bread. Press the sandwich down
firmly and sauté it in butter over low heat. When one
side is brown and the cheese somewhat melted, turn

the sandwich over with a spatula and brown the other side. Cut it into strips and serve immediately.

Note: An interesting variation is to add chopped green or black olives or, if you prefer, bits of pimento between the ham and cheese. If you use pimento, do not use cayenne pepper; black pepper is better.

MELON AND PROSCIUTTO

You are probably familiar with the combination of melon and Prosciutto as a first course for lunch or dinner, and if the melon is good—something that can never be taken for granted—it is excellent. Incidentally, I do not go along with those who feel that freshly ground black pepper adds anything to what I believe to be a perfect marriage of the delicately pungent and the delicately bland; after all, Prosciutto is not without flavor. Appropriate as it is for a first course, this admirable combination is equally good as a pre-dinner accompaniment to drinks or as one of the items one might serve at a cocktail party. The latter cases call for a smaller scale, of course.

The melon should be cut into any shape except a cube; nothing is less appetizing than food cut into cubes. I don't know why this should be, but I suspect that, contrary to the views of Monsieur Cézanne, the cube is not a natural form (except possibly in rock formations, which to date have nothing to do with food).

INGREDIENTS

melon, preferably Spanish

Prosciutto

To make: I suggest that you cut the melon into small wedges one inch in width at the thick end and one and one-half inches in length. The best melons for this purpose are Spanish melons, but any other melon of good quality will do. Buy Prosciutto from a dealer who cuts it paper thin—not for reasons of economy, but of flavor. Remove some of the outside fat from the Prosciutto and set it aside (it is useful for sautéing vegetables), wrap the Prosciutto around each melon wedge, and fasten it with a toothpick.

To serve: For obvious reasons, this should not be prepared too far in advance of serving. Have a pepper grinder available for the conformists.

PÂTÉ OF BREAST OF CHICKEN
WITH TARRAGON

Of the various pâtés I make, I believe pâté of breast of chicken with tarragon is the most delicate, both in flavor and appearance. A distinct advantage is that its solid ingredients are readily available in every butcher shop and relatively inexpensive. The pâté may be served simply in its terrine or, more elegantly, in aspic, unmolded on a bed of lettuce. In any case, it keeps well in the refrigerator, if you should be fortunate enough to have some left over. The number of people this pâté will serve depends on how it is used; as part of a buffet, the following recipe will serve forty. It should be sliced thin, which is how it tastes best.

INGREDIENTS

1 lb veal of a not-too-expensive cut (shank, for example), ground twice

1 lb ground pork (Unseasoned pork sausage meat will do.)

2 lb chicken breasts (Bone the breasts, reject the skin, and cut the meat into long, 3/4 inch strips. If you end up with some small bits of chicken, add them to the ground veal.)

6 shallots or 1 bunch scallions (with some of the green part), finely chopped

2 egg yolks

1/8 tsp leaf thyme

1 bay leaf

1/4 Tbsp dried tarragon

1/2 lb fresh fatback (If not available fresh, buy the same quantity of salt pork.)

salt and pepper (If salt pork is used, be careful with the salt.)

2 ounces large pistachio nuts (Shell them and remove the skin by rubbing with a rough towel. It isn't necessary to remove every bit of the skin.)

3 cups beef bouillon

1 1/2 cups not-too-dry white wine (Graves or sauterne)

3 jiggers bourbon whiskey

1/3 cup dry Madeira wine

1 1/2 envelopes gelatine

To make: In a large bowl mix the veal, pork, shallots, thyme, one-fourth tablespoon tarragon, salt, pepper, one cup white wine, and two jiggers whiskey. Set aside for one hour, mixing thoroughly every fifteen minutes. In another bowl marinate the strips of chicken in one-half cup white wine and one jigger whiskey. Set aside for one hour, tossing the meat in the marinade from time to time.

Slice the fatback as thin as possible. Do not use the rind. (If you must use salt pork, put it in boiling water, reduce heat, and blanch for ten minutes to get rid of most of the salt. Remove and cool under running water. Slice as thin as possible, rejecting the rind.) Mix the two egg yolks into the ground meat mixture, at first with a spoon, then with oiled hands. During the mixing, add any liquid that will drain off the marinating chicken strips.

A proper oval-shaped terrine is ideal for this pâté, but few people have one. In any case, I believe it is best to use a round, ovenproof glass or earthenware dish, not too shallow. A two-quart soufflé dish is perfect.

Preheat the oven to 350°. Line the mold (dish) with the slices of fatback, taking particular care that the bottom is well covered. Add a layer of ground meat, then a layer of chicken strips. Run the chicken strips in the same direction each time, keeping track of this direction. (The cooked pâté is sliced at right angles to the direction in which the chicken pieces run, which gives a sort of mosaic appearance to each slice. The bay leaf is placed on top of the completely assembled, uncooked pâté to indicate, rather like an arrow, the direction in which the chicken strips run.) Add one-third of the pistachio nuts, spreading them out evenly. Then add another layer of the ground meat, pressing

The pâté in its terrine (below) as it looks after it has been cooked and allowed to cool under weights. The residual fat is quite visible. The bay leaf on the top of the pâté is fresh—picked from a tree my wife cultivates, along with many other plants and herbs, in our apartment. The cloth under the terrine is a placemat handworked by Alice B. Toklas.

The pâté removed from the terrine (top right) and divested of the fatback lining and the fat rendered during cooking. The terrine has been washed and now contains the Madeira-flavored aspic which will garnish the pâté.

The pâté prepared for serving (bottom right). A slice has been cut from the end to show the white, inner layer of chicken breast as well as the truffle-and-pistachio interlarding. The leafy garnish is watercress.

down firmly to fill the spaces between the chicken strips. Continue in this sequence until all the ground meat, chicken strips, and pistachio nuts are used up, taking care to end with a layer of ground meat. Put the bay leaf on top as indicated above and put the mold in another dish or pan containing three inches of water. Cover the mold with foil and put the mold in its water bath in a preheated oven. Cook at 350° for one hour and forty-five minutes. Remove the foil from the mold and inspect the melted fat around the meat. If it is perfectly clear, the pâté is done. If it is at all cloudy, cook without the foil for fifteen minutes more or until the fat becomes clear.

When done, remove the terrine, still in its water bath, to a counter. The next step explains why I prefer a round mold for the pâté. Take a plate, just a bit smaller than the inner circumference of the mold and place it on top of the pâté. Balance a board (a bread board, for example) on the plate and pile as many heavy cans of food as you can on it without danger of the whole apparatus falling. While you are doing this a good deal of fat will spill over into the water bath. Don't be alarmed. Leave the pâté this way overnight. The next morning, lift the terrine from the water bath, clean the sides and bottom with hot water, and put the pâté in the refrigerator.

To serve: The pâté, when thoroughly chilled, will be firm and somewhat shrunken from the sides of the mold. There will be some surface fat around the sides, but underneath will be excellent meat jelly. Remove the fat—or not, as you wish—and serve the pâté from the vessel, cutting it in thin slices against the grain.

You may remove the pâté from the mold and coat it with aspic as follows.

INGREDIENTS FOR THE ASPIC

1¼ *Tbsp dried tarragon*

3 *cups strong beef bouillon*

⅓ *cup dry Madeira wine*

1½ *envelopes gelatine*

To make: Remove all fat from the pâté, including the vestiges of the fatback lining. Some pieces of the fatback will be imbedded in the pâté, but don't worry about marring its appearance; the aspic will cover all that. Set aside the natural jelly and clean out the terrine. To make the aspic, cook the natural jelly, beef bouillon, and tarragon for fifteen minutes. Strain and add the Madeira wine and the gelatine. Stir until the gelatine is thoroughly dissolved. Put a one-inch layer of aspic in the terrine and chill to set. When it is firm, place the pâté on it, bay leaf-side down. Pour the rest of the somewhat chilled aspic around the sides to the top. Refrigerate until set. To unmold, loosen the sides with a knife, dip the mold in hot water, place the serving dish on top of the pâté, and turn pâté and plate over so that the pâté falls onto the plate.

To serve: Surround the pâté with lettuce leaves.

Note: If you feel like splurging a bit, use truffles in this pâté instead of pistachio nuts, or use truffles and one-half the amount of pistachio nuts. The smallest available can of truffles (slightly over one ounce) will do, but a slightly larger can is better. Cut the truffles in strips and form a single continuous strip in the center of the pâté, so that each slice will have its share. The

deep black of the truffles makes a nice contrast to the
ivory color of the chicken.

RICE SALAD

The Japanese appreciate cold rice mixed with bits of
fish, meats, or vegetables and flavored with vinegar.
This rice salad, though, is not at all oriental. If it had
to be categorized, I would call it Mediterranean Grand
Hotel.

A well-made rice salad is a perfect summer buffet dish
—tasty, delicate, and colorful as a mosaic. It is a flexible
salad, but not a catchall for leftovers. All sorts of combinations are possible, but in each case the salad should
be based on one main ingredient—for example, the
breast meat of poached or roasted chicken, poached
lobster, shrimp, crab meat, breast of game birds (not
duck), or best-quality tuna fish (canned in olive oil).
Strong-flavored ingredients, such as lamb, sardines, and
broccoli, must be avoided.

All the firm ingredients (not parsley or other herbs)
should be cut neatly and uniformly, and no piece should
be larger than a small pea or—better yet—the size of a
pine nut. The rice should be thoroughly cooked, but
firm, with each grain separate.

The best way to cook rice for salad is in the Italian
fashion. For five cups of rice, heat an eight-quart pot
of salted water. When the water is boiling, pour the
rice into it a little at a time so that the boiling continues. If you use unprocessed rice, wash it very well in
many waters until no trace of starch is visible on the
surface of the water. Cook until the rice is tender, but
not mushy. The infallible test is to squeeze a grain of

rice between your thumb and forefinger, or, if you are a taster, to test a grain with your teeth. When done, the rice should be firm, but unresistant to your fingers or teeth. Drain the rice well in a colander and allow to cool.

For the sauce—for the salad does have a sauce—use either a vinaigrette (see p. 29) or homemade mayonnaise (see p. 26). Use just enough to lightly bind the mixture.

The following are a few of the possible combinations. Each choice gives ingredients for eight when the salad is part of a mixed hors d'oeuvre.

WITH CHICKEN

5 cups rice, cooked

¾ cup cooked white meat of chicken, chopped

½ cup very small peas, cooked

2 Tbsp pine nuts (pignoli)

1 Tbsp small currants, soaked in white wine

⅕ cup well-drained black olives, washed in cold water and finely chopped

2 Tbsp pimento, finely chopped

2 hard-boiled egg yolks, chopped

1 Tbsp parsley, very, very finely chopped

¾ to 1 cup vinaigrette sauce or mayonnaise

WITH LOBSTER

5 cups rice, cooked

¾ cup poached lobster, chopped

1 Tbsp chives

3 Tbsp tomato, peeled, seeded, and chopped

½ cup very small peas

1 tsp fresh tarragon, chopped (if available)

1 Tbsp green olives, very finely chopped

⅙ tsp cayenne pepper

¾ to 1 cup vinaigrette sauce or mayonnaise

WITH TUNA

5 cups rice, cooked

¾ cup white tuna, chopped

1 Tbsp capers

½ cup green beans, cooked and chopped

½ cup tomato, peeled, seeded, and chopped

2 Tbsp black olives, washed and chopped

1 Tbsp chives, chopped

¾ to 1 cup vinaigrette sauce or mayonnaise

WITH SHRIMP

5 cups rice, cooked

¾ cup poached shrimp, chopped

½ cup mushrooms sautéed in oil, chopped

½ cup small peas

1 Tbsp chives, chopped

2 Tbsp pimento, chopped

1 Tbsp black olives, chopped

¾ to 1 cup vinaigrette sauce or mayonnaise

The following go well in rice salad:

white meat of turkey	tomatoes, peeled, seeded,
white meat of chicken	and chopped
breast of quail	pine nuts
breast of partridge	almonds, slivered
breast of pheasant	currants, small
firm white fish, poached	green peppers, peeled
lobster	pimentos, peeled
shrimp	yellow peppers, peeled
crab meat	Italian peppers, peeled
boiled ham	zucchini
Prosciutto	black olives
Westphalian ham	green olives
tuna, canned in olive oil	capers
black truffles	parsley
white truffles	fresh tarragon
mushrooms	fresh dill
artichoke hearts	chives
green beans	chervil

VEAL AND HAM PÂTÉ

The blandness of veal and the definite flavor of ham, when combined with cognac, Madeira, dry white wine, and shallots, produces something far better than its parts. It is unlike the God-knows-how-many versions of *pâté de campagne* and *pâté maison,* which are best served in thick slices with *cornichons* (sour pickles). This pâté should be sliced thin and served on buttered toast or buttered bread as a cocktail accompaniment or pre-dinner appetizer. However, dressed up with aspic and sliced in moderately thick slices, it provides an elegant first course for lunch or dinner. When presented as a first course, the following recipe will serve ten; as part of a buffet or cocktail accompaniment the pâté will serve forty to fifty people.

INGREDIENTS

1¼ lb lean, boiled ham, ⅓ inch thick, cut into
¼ inch strips

1¼ lb absolutely lean veal, cut in strips, as above

1 lb veal (shank, for example), ground twice

1 lb pork, ground twice (Good-quality unseasoned
sausage meat will do.)

freshly ground black pepper, to taste

6 shallots or 8 scallions (the white part only), very
finely chopped

2 eggs, lightly beaten

¼ tsp leaf thyme

1 Tbsp parsley, very finely chopped

1 large, well-formed bay leaf

¾ lb fatback of pork (This is the cut used for
salt pork, but it is available fresh. However, if
you have difficulty finding the fresh product, buy
the same quantity salt pork, wash it in warm
water, and blanch it in boiling water for ten minutes to rid it of excess salt. Allow it to cool. In any
case, fresh or not, slice it as thin as possible and
set aside.)

½ cup cognac

½ cup dry Madeira wine

½ cup dry white wine (or, at any rate, a not-too-
sweet wine)

To make: Put the ham and veal strips in a bowl and add the cognac, Madeira, and white wine. Set aside for at least one hour. Then drain the liquid from the strips into another bowl, add all the other ingredients except the whole bay leaf to the liquid, and mix very well.

To construct the pâté, line the bottom and sides of a glass or porcelain dish, large enough to accommodate all the ingredients comfortably, with the thin slices of fatback. With some of the liquid-ground meat mixture (*farce*) make a firm layer on the bottom of the dish. Add a layer of veal and ham strips, alternating them symmetrically. (From here on, pay attention to the direction in which you line up the meat strips; they should run in the same direction, so that when the pâté is sliced—against the grain of the strips—the slices will present a mosaic effect. The reserved bay leaf is embedded in the top layer of the pâté to indicate the direction in which the meat strips run and, consequently, the direction in which to slice the pâté.) Add another layer of the *farce*, then another layer of strips, and continue in this fashion until both strips and *farce* have been used up. End with a layer of the *farce*. In preparing the layers of strips and *farce*, take care to press down well; the whole thing should be quite firm. Put the bay leaf on top to indicate the direction in which the meat strips run. If there is even a drop of liquid left in the bowl, pour it on the meat; the liquid has a great deal to do with making this pâté what it is.

Preheat the oven to 350°. Cover the dish with aluminum foil, put it in a pan with enough water to reach to half the height of the terrine, and bake for one hour and forty-five minutes. Then remove the foil and inspect the fat surrounding the pâté, which will have shrunk somewhat. If the fat is absolutely clear, the pâté is done. If the fat is at all cloudy, cook the pâté uncovered for fifteen minutes more or until the fat becomes clear. When the pâté is done, take it from the oven, leaving it in its water bath. Put a plate that just fits the interior of the pâté dish on top of the meat. Then, in any way you can devise, put weights on top of the plate, but don't overdo it. The object is to hold the pâté firm while to cools, but too much weight will squeeze out the flavorful meat juices. While you are doing this, a good deal of fat will flow over the terrine into the water bath (which is why it is there). Pay no attention. Allow the pâté to cool, preferably overnight, and then put it in the refrigerator. If you wish, serve the pâté directly from the terrine in which it was cooked. The French very often do, and there is the advantage that, sealed in its fat, the pâté will keep very well in the refrigerator for at least a week.

The French also serve the pâté in aspic, which is much more elegant. Here is how it is done.

INGREDIENTS

ham and veal pâté

1¼ envelopes gelatin

2 cups chicken or beef bouillon

*½ cup not-too-dry white wine, dry Madeira wine,
or not-too-sweet port (imported)*

parsley sprigs

To make: When it has been thoroughly chilled in the refrigerator, take the pâté from its receptacle and carefully remove and reject all the congealed fat as well as the vestiges of the fatback. Some bits of the fatback may be embedded in the pâté. Remove them, even if it seems that you might mar the appearance of the pâté; those parts will not be noticeable when they are coated with aspic. To make the aspic, dissolve the gelatin in one-half cup of cold chicken or beef bouillon. Bring one and one-half cups chicken or beef bouillon to a boil, mix in the softened gelatin, and stir until it is thoroughly dissolved. Remove from the heat and add the white wine, Madeira, or port. Clean the receptacle in which the pâté was cooked and add enough aspic to form a one-half-inch layer on the bottom. Chill until firm. Place the pâté in the receptacle, but topside (with the bay leaf) down. Add the rest of the aspic, which should just reach the top (which was the bottom) of the pâté. Refrigerate until firm. Loosen the sides with a knife dipped in hot water. Set the bottom of the dish in hot water for a few seconds, put a plate over the top, and turn plate and pâté dish over so that the pâté can fall onto the plate. If the pâté refuses to budge, dip a cloth into very hot water, wring it out quickly, and place it on the bottom of the pâté dish. Repeat until the aspic-covered pâté falls onto the plate.

To serve: Surround the pâté with sprigs of parsley. If served as a first course, cut the pâté in fairly thick slices. If served as a snack with drinks or as part of a cocktail party buffet, slice it thin.

BAKED RED ONIONS

For baked red onions, choose very firm onions. If they are the least bit soft, have nothing to do with them; they will lack flavor, texture, and color. As with baking potatoes, they should as nearly as possible be of the same size. Do not trim or peel the onions until after they are cooked. Incidentally, onions cooked in this fashion are very digestible. When served as part of a mixed hors d'oeuvre or buffet lunch or dinner, the ingredients below will serve six.

INGREDIENTS FOR SIX

6 medium red onions

3 Tbsp water

1 Tbsp olive oil

FOR THE SAUCE

4 Tbsp olive oil

3 tsp red wine vinegar

¼ tsp dried leaf oregano

salt and pepper

1 tsp parsley, very finely chopped

Note: For this dish, a specialty of Provence, red onions are best, but any other variety of onion (including Spanish or Bermuda onions, if they are not too large) may be used.

To make: Preheat the oven to 350°. Put the onions in an ovenproof pan or dish into which you have poured the water and olive oil. Put the pan or dish into the oven and cook until tender, which will take approximately one hour. If you have any doubts (and from my experience a good many people should doubt the temperature of their ovens), cut into one of the onions with a very sharp knife—a procedure natural to any good chef. When they are thoroughly cooked but not disintegrating, take the onions from the oven and set aside until they are cool enough to handle, which does not mean cold. This onion salad should be served tepid, so the onions must be peeled while warm. Onions, like potatoes, manage to incorporate the sauce more satisfactorily when they are mixed with it while still warm. Peel and slice the onions, mix in all the other ingredients, and serve immediately.

During the cooking process a certain amount of juice will be forced from the onions into the pan, which is why the water and oil are used. If the water dries up completely and the juice is about to carmelize, add a little more water.

To serve: Serve baked red onions for lunch with cold ham, pâté, cold roast beef, tongue, tomatoes in a vinaigrette sauce, or cold boiled beef.

MEATBALLS IN MADEIRA SAUCE

Meatballs in Madeira sauce have nothing to do with Italian, Swedish, or any other national meatballs. They contain nothing but good-quality ground beef, egg yolks, grated onion, very finely chopped parsley, dried basil, salt, and pepper. They taste like meat. The sauce, which helps a good deal, is somewhat more sophisticated.

Since they are very small, the meatballs are ideal for a cocktail party, served hot from a chafing dish with buttered slices of party rye (small, pre-sliced, packaged rye bread) served on the side. If you think there is something unhandy about fishing meatballs from a hot sauce and placing them on small slices of bread, don't fret. I have seen thousands of these meatballs consumed without accident. When the meatballs are served as part of a selection of snacks at a cocktail party, they will serve twenty people.

INGREDIENTS FOR TWENTY

2 lb very lean round steak, ground twice

butter, as needed

1 large red or yellow onion

2 egg yolks

1 Tbsp parsley, very finely chopped

½ tsp dried basil

salt and pepper

FOR THE SAUCE

3 cups rich beef bouillon

½ cup dry Madeira wine

1½ tsp butter

1½ tsp flour

salt and pepper

To make: Mix the ground beef with the parsley, basil, salt, and pepper. Peel the onion and grate it onto the mixture, being careful not to lose any of the onion juice. Add the two egg yolks and mix well, at first with a spoon, then with your hands. Now, with oiled hands form small meatballs about the size of a hazelnut. This recipe makes a lot of meatballs, and it becomes something of a problem to find room for them, particularly since they should not touch each other. My best solution is to put the meatballs on a number of sheets of waxed paper, which, if necessary, can be stacked on top of each other.

In a large low-sided skillet brown the meatballs in batches, being careful to avoid crowding. As each batch is browned (each meatball on all sides), put it into a bowl and start on a new batch. Even if you have used very lean beef, a certain amount of fat and meat juice will be rendered during the browning of the meatballs. Pour this off and reject it as it accumulates, adding more butter as needed.

The last step is to make the sauce. Prepare a roux of the butter and flour, cooking it over medium heat until it browns. Stir constantly to prevent it from burning. Add the heated beef stock to the roux, little by little, stirring constantly to make a smooth mixture. Lower the heat, add the meatballs and the Madeira wine, and cook over very low heat for one hour. If the stock and wine mixture does not almost cover the meatballs, add more stock. Before serving, skim the excess fat from the surface of the sauce.

Note: The roux—the thickening element in the sauce— is a light one, which I prefer. If you like more body to the sauce, add more flour and butter.

QUICHE LORRAINE

The popular dish *quiche Lorraine* originated in Lorraine, one of the northern provinces of France, but it has since done a good deal of traveling, not all of it in first-class. I have tasted versions in New York that reminded me of nothing so much as the dreadful mixture known as a western sandwich—onions, green pepper, ham, and eggs. However, there are many quite acceptable variations, including *quiche Provençal* with tomatoes and others made with spinach, crab meat, lobster, onions, or mushrooms. Undoubtedly there are some variations I don't know about and about which I am not overly curious. The only version I am giving is the original, which consists of ham (I prefer Canadian bacon), heavy cream, pepper, and whole eggs. It does not include cheese. What makes this *quiche* good is the puff paste crust, which lifts the dish into another category altogether.

INGREDIENTS FOR FIVE TO SIX

4 large eggs

1 pint heavy cream

6 or 7 ounces lean boiled ham or Canadian bacon, cut in strips 1 inch long and ½ inch wide

3 Tbsp butter

pepper (No salt is needed; the ham or bacon provides enough.)

puff paste (see p. 227)

To make: Preheat the oven to 450°. Roll out the crust, making sure to roll the part that forms the bottom crust very thin. Place in an eight-inch pie dish or pan, somewhat deeper than the common type. See that the dough extends, and without pulling, well beyond the edges of the pan or dish, after tucking it down well in the pan. Sauté the ham or bacon lightly in butter. Distribute the bits of ham or bacon evenly on the dough on the bottom of the pan, and add the butter left in the sautéing pan. In a bowl beat the cream, eggs, and pepper until thoroughly blended, and a little more. If the heavy cream is aerated enough, but not whipped, it will make a more soufflé-like custard filling. Pour this over the ham or bacon, and bake the *quiche* for ten minutes in a 450° oven. Lower the heat to 400° and bake for ten minutes more. If, at this point, the pastry is browning well and the filling is still quite soft, reduce the heat to 300° and continue baking until the filling is just set (remember that it will continue to cook after it is taken from the oven).

To serve: *Quiche* is best when served tepid, and it does reheat very well. Reheat in a low oven, around 250°, to avoid overbrowning the crust.

EGGS

IF THERE IS an item in the kitchen more versatile than the egg, I don't know what it is. Its roles run the gamut from the mundane—a plain fried egg, for example—to the exalted—the soul and substance of a beautiful souffle and an important participating ingredient in a baked Alaska. What we do neglect, I believe, are the more than four hundred ways of preparing eggs which in complexity and elegance lie between the extremes mentioned above. Have you ever tasted creamy scrambled eggs served in a heated and hollowed-out brioche or an egg in aspic—not commercial aspic but one made from a fine stock flavored with Madeira or port wine? Neither of these is difficult to make; and, as for the elegance of eggs in aspic, I have in front of me two menus—one from Maxim's in Paris and the other from Larue—and eggs in aspic are featured in both.

SCRAMBLED EGGS

Properly scrambled eggs are virtually unknown in the United States. One very large and well-known restaurant chain serves only powdered scrambled eggs—a fact that rubs out printable comment. Obviously one does better at the local lunch counter, where one can see the eggs being cracked. The trouble with lunch counters, however, is that their cooks are just as pressed for time as the powdered-egg people, which means that the eggs get a stir or two in passing. The result is usually something resembling an egg cake, although to be kind one might refer to it as a sort of modified *frittata*. There is only one correct method for cooking scrambled eggs: cook them over low heat while continuously stirring with a wooden spoon. For practical purposes that means that they can be made properly only at home. Properly prepared, scrambled eggs are smooth and creamy. They do not need the addition of cream, milk, or any other liquid. What is required are fresh eggs, fresh butter, salt, pepper, and a little patience. The reward is the knowledge that you are serving a dish that has been raised to the level of a luxury, solely because of your skill and patience.

SCRAMBLED EGGS WITH BACON

If you like crisp bacon, you will like these scrambled eggs. The bacon, chopped very fine, is fried until crisp and drained of every bit of fat. In other words, you have flavor and texture without bulk. Too, the flavor is mellow instead of sharp. This is an ideal brunch dish, especially when served with very crisply toasted English muffins.

INGREDIENTS FOR SIX

1½ lb first-quality lean bacon, finely chopped

18 eggs, lightly but thoroughly beaten

pepper

2 Tbsp butter

9 English muffins, grilled on both sides under a broiler, and very well buttered

apricot jelly or preserves

To make: Fry the bacon until crisp. This can only be done by pouring off the fat as it renders, and there will be a good deal of it. The trick is to achieve bacon completely rendered of fat—crisp, but not carbonized. When done, spread the bacon on paper towels and dry very well. Beat the eggs, and add the bacon bits and pepper. Over low heat melt the butter and start the cooking, which, as you will learn, takes a bit of time. To the extent that you take time, however, the better the eggs will be. Stir constantly with a wooden spoon, paying particular attention to the bottom of the pan. Don't lose patience. The eggs should thicken without forming lumps. Don't forget that eggs continue to cook for a while after they are removed from heat.

To serve: Put the crisp muffin halves on plates and pour the eggs over them as neatly as possible. Have apricot jelly or preserves available on the table for those who like it.

OMELETS

A great deal can be said for omelets: they are tasty, they look nice on a plate, they can be made in precise individual portions, and they take no time at all to make. However, they cannot be made without a proper pan—a pan used only for omelets, which is never washed in soap or hot water, but is instead thoroughly wiped with paper towels. Pans of this type are not expensive (see p. 2).

Omelets are ideal for late breakfast or early lunch because they go well with so many other foods and garnishes—such as mushrooms, spinach, sorrel, ham, lobster, caviar, truffles, sautéed potatoes, and artichoke hearts. Conceivable garnishes for omelets number over one hundred.

Clearly, it is worth knowing how to make an omelet. Here is how I do it. Using two or three eggs to an omelet, beat the eggs (to which you have added salt and pepper) with a fork or hand beater, but only until the yolks and whites are thoroughly blended. Add one tablespoon butter to the pan and cook it over high heat, lifting and twisting the pan so that the butter covers the sides as well as the bottom, until just slightly browned, or at the stage the French call *noisette* (hazelnut color). Immediately pour in the eggs. Wait a few seconds (no more) to allow the eggs to catch or set on the bottom; then, tilting the pan by lifting the handle up, with a spatula nudge the eggs on the highest part downwards. When the firm part slides down, immediately tilt the pan in the other direction. Continue this sequence until the eggs have just about set, but not too firmly. Then, with the spatula fold the half closer to you (and the pan's handle) over the farther half.

Cook for a few seconds more to brown the bottom (which will become the top); then with a quick movement turn the pan right over, gently depositing the omelet on a plate.

Keep in mind that the omelet will continue to cook for a while after you put it on the plate. A good omelet should be light golden in color and soft in its inside.

VEGETABLE OMELET GARNISH

Vegetable omelet garnish is an apt enough name for this mixture, since it contains a number of firm ingredients, but the dish is actually half garnish and half sauce. It is cooked in stages in one utensil so that the garnish and the sauce blend and the natural juices of the vegetables, as well as the stock and wines, contribute to the flavor.

INGREDIENTS FOR FOUR THREE-EGG OMELETS

2 bunches scallions (with half the green parts), cleaned and chopped

4 medium tomatoes, peeled, seeded, and chopped

2 packages frozen artichoke hearts

½ cup beef or chicken stock

½ cup dry white wine

¼ cup dry Madeira wine (dry sherry is a good substitute)

½ tsp dried or 1 Tbsp fresh tarragon

3 Tbsp olive oil

salt and pepper

To make: Heat the oil in a heavy-bottomed skillet. Add the chopped scallions and cook over low heat until they are transparent, but not brown. Add the chopped tomatoes to the scallions and cook for ten minutes. Then add the frozen artichoke hearts, raise the heat, and cook until the artichokes are separated. Add the stock, wines, salt, pepper, and tarragon. Cover the skillet and cook over the lowest heat until the artichokes are tender and the sauce is well blended and somewhat thick.

To serve: Prepare the sauce or garnish in advance and keep it hot. Cook the omelets and pour the garnish over them. Vegetable omelet garnish also goes well with grilled or fried fish, grilled or roasted lamb, and sautéed chicken.

POACHED EGGS

A perfectly poached egg, just firm enough to maintain its shape with the yolk soft and runny, is a fine thing, equally good hot or cold. For breakfast hot eggs are mandatory, but I think a poached egg is best when cold—garnished, sauced, or as part of a composed dish —and mouth-watering when set in a tarragon-flavored wine aspic with bits of ham and tomato and a few blanched tarragon leaves inlaid in the jelly.

Except for its shape, a poached egg differs very little from a coddled egg, but the difference is important. A soft coddled egg is an egg cooked in its shell, but only until it is firm enough to be peeled. A poached egg, flat on one side, tends to stay where you put it; a coddled egg has a tendency to roll. A coddled egg, if properly cooked, is having all it can do to hold itself together and is difficult to handle. If this isn't clear, try peeling and handling six coddled eggs when you are in a hurry. I also find that a cold poached egg tastes better than a cold coddled egg, or seems to, and I think I know why. A poached egg, because of the method of cooking, is perforce trimmed of some of its white; a coddled egg has too much white to my taste.

To make: There are several ways of poaching eggs. This is the method I prefer. Fill a two-quart enameled, stainless steel, or glass pot to an inch from the top with water. Add one teaspoon of salt, and bring the water to a boil. When the water is boiling, crack a chilled, fresh egg into a saucer. With a perforated spoon, stir the water in a circular motion. (The object of the motion is to prevent the egg from settling on the bottom and sticking.) Very quickly turn down the heat and slide the egg into the water. Turn the heat up again until the water is just boiling, but not too actively. Too much activity in the water when the egg is still soft will cause the white to disintegrate or shred. When the egg white is opaque, lift the egg carefully with a perforated spoon. If it sits firmly, it is done (don't forget that an egg continues to cook after it is removed from the water). Two or more eggs can be poached at a time. I have poached as many as ten eggs at a time, so don't be intimidated. However, before each egg is added to the water, stir the water with a circular motion and regulate the heat as indicated above.

Poached eggs are not as fragile as they seem. But if they must be handled to any degree—other than putting them on a plate or on toast—they should be allowed to cook until somewhat firm, although the yolks should still be runny. Some chefs advise adding a little vinegar to the water for poaching eggs, but I have found that this does not make the slightest difference. What does make a difference is the freshness of the eggs. A not-too-fresh egg will tend to separate, the white falling away from the yolk, which is not appetizing. To make poached eggs in advance to be served hot, keep them at a good serving temperature by putting them into warm but not hot water; that is the way restaurants do it.

MOUILLETES

Mouilletes—crusty fingers of fried white bread—go well with breakfast or brunch soft-boiled eggs.

To make: Cut firm white bread into finger lengths about one-half-inch thick, remove crusts, dip in milk, and fry in deep oil just until a pale golden color (a matter of a few seconds). Drain the bread on paper towels.

To serve: Serve in a folded napkin with soft-boiled eggs in egg-cups—the large ends of the eggs up. The *mouilletes* are eaten dipped in the egg yolks, to which have been added butter, salt, and pepper.

Note: A curious fact about *mouilletes* is that we know precisely how they looked over three hundred years ago, as they form part of the composition in a number of still-life paintings of the seventeenth and eighteenth century. *Mouilletes* are still regular fare in Spain and in certain regions of France, notably in Périgord.

[87]

FISH

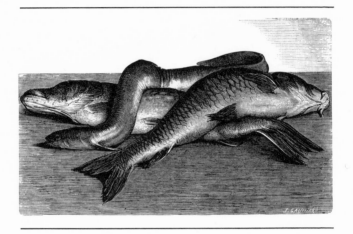

SOME PEOPLE are so fond of fish they could eat it every day; others put up with it when it is served to them; a few can't eat it at all. It's curious that these tastes have little to do with geography. I know people brought up in coastal towns and cities who simply won't touch fish; and the two most enthusiastic fish eaters I know were born respectively in Salt Lake City and Toronto, Canada.

Fish is a very healthful food. It contains but a fraction of the fat contained in meat and is virtually without cholesterol. This wouldn't mean much, however, if it didn't taste good. Few things are more appetizing than a poached salmon with an appropriate sauce; and few dishes are as delicate as a grilled trout with a little butter and a plain boiled potato.

As with all foods, everything depends on one's source of supply, and this is even more important with fish, which is highly perishable. As always, the best way to be certain in such matters is to locate the best shop, give it your custom and your confidence, and, even though it may be expensive, in the long run you will save money.

BROILED SWORDFISH

One of the specialties of the Turkish cuisine (which, by the way, is a good deal more sophisticated than certain other Middle Eastern and Levantine cuisines) is swordfish, cut into pieces, brushed with oil, and cooked on a spit over a charcoal fire. The Turks do not interlard preparations cooked in this way with bacon, as is the European fashion. With swordfish, they put a bay leaf between each piece of fish. The remaining seasoning is simply salt, pepper, and lemon juice.

INGREDIENTS FOR SIX

2½ to 3 lb swordfish, sliced into 6 steaks

3 medium bay leaves, roughly crushed

½ tsp leaf thyme, crushed and dried

olive oil

2 lemons, quartered

salt and pepper

To make: Brush the steaks with olive oil, sprinkle with crushed bay leaves, and dust lightly with crushed thyme leaves. Put the slices on a grill and cook under the broiler, turning once, until done, which will not take long, although the length of time will depend on the heat of the broiler and the thickness of the slices. To be quite certain the fish is cooked through, cut into one of the larger slices and see if the flesh flakes easily. If so, it is done. Do not overcook swordfish or it will be dry. Add salt and pepper before serving the steaks.

To serve: Serve with rice into which you have mixed sautéed zucchini. Pass quartered lemons, from which you have removed the seeds.

BROILED SCALLOPS

These broiled scallops are coated with fine bread crumbs, but no flour or egg is used. The result is extremely appetizing because the flavor is not masked by a heavy crust. In fact, prepared this way, scallops are as light as a feather.

INGREDIENTS FOR FOUR

bread crumbs, dried but not toasted

2 lb scallops (If they are large, cut them in half against the grain. If they are overly moist, dry them quickly with paper towels, place them on a grill in one layer, and set them aside for thirty minutes. Do not cover them.)

½ cup olive oil or more, if needed

salt and pepper

2 lemons for garnishing

tartar sauce

To make: Put the olive oil in a bowl. Add the scallops, tossing them with a spoon to be sure they are well coated with oil on all sides. Remove the scallops from the oil and drain them over the bowl from which they were removed. Reserve the oil. Spread some bread crumbs mixed with salt and pepper on a piece of waxed paper. Place the scallops on top of the crumbs and mix them lightly with your hands, making sure that each scallop is well covered with crumbs on all sides. Put the scallops, one by one, on a doubled sheet of heavy aluminum foil, leaving a little space between each one. Put them under the broiler and cook until lightly browned, turning each scallop once. When they have been turned over, sprinkle them with the oil you have held in reserve. Do this as uniformly as possible, even if it amounts to applying only a few drops to each scallop.

To serve: Serve with tartar sauce, French-fried potatoes (see p. 201), and a lettuce and tomato salad.

BROILED WHOLE RED SNAPPER OR SEA BASS

The advantage of this cooking method for broiled whole red snapper or sea bass, quite aside from the fine flavor and perfect texture it produces, is that the fish does not have to be turned. The only handling is in transferring the cooked fish to a serving platter. Don't worry about the fish cooking uniformly; given the structure of a red snapper or a sea bass, the fish comes out just right. Any fish—sea or fresh-water—of a shape similar to red snapper or sea bass, including trout, may be cooked in this way.

INGREDIENTS FOR THREE

*1 4-lb red snapper or sea bass, preferably with
the head left on*

2 to 3 Tbsp fine flour or cornstarch

¼ tsp thyme

⅛ tsp rosemary, crushed or ground in a pepper mill

salt and pepper

6 ounces butter, melted

juice of ½ lemon

2 lemons, cut in quarters

olive oil

To make: Broil the fish on a doubled piece of aluminum foil well coated with olive oil, to facilitate sliding the cooked fish onto a serving platter. Place the fish, *skin-side up* (the fish is spread and somewhat flattened by pressing down on its backbone), on the foil and coat it with olive oil, using a piece of paper towel as a brush. Mix the thyme, rosemary, salt, and pepper into the flour and dust the fish uniformly with the mixture. Place the fish under the broiler, at least six inches from a medium-hot broiler flame, and cook for twenty-five minutes. To determine if the fish is done, insert a knife into its thickest part. If the flesh is white and flaky, it is ready; if not, broil for a few minutes longer.

To serve: Garnish with quarters of lemon. Serve with the melted butter and lemon juice mixed together and, if possible, kept warm with a candle-heater under the sauce-boat. Boiled new potatoes, sprinkled with very,

very finely chopped parsley, are an ideal accompaniment.

SOLE À LA DUGLÈRE

There is a tradition that fish prepared *à la Duglère* is sliced. But as Prosper Motagne (whom I consider the greatest chef France has produced) said, "This doesn't make much sense with sole," and obviously it does not with other flat fish, such as gray sole or flounder. I advise you to cut each fillet—of which there are four to a fish—in half diagonally. Again, square cut should be avoided; it would tend to look like an economy measure, which is never desirable.

INGREDIENTS FOR FOUR

2 lb fillets of gray sole, flounder, red snapper, or striped bass

¼ cup dry white wine

4 medium tomatoes, peeled, seeded, and chopped

1 medium onion, finely chopped

⅕ tsp leaf thyme

piece of bay leaf, the size of a dime

5 Tbsp butter, chopped

salt and pepper

1 tsp parsley, very finely chopped

1 Tbsp flour

2½ Tbsp water

lemons, quartered

To make: Preheat the oven to 350°. In an ovenproof glass or earthenware dish, make a bed of the tomatoes, onion, thyme, bay leaf, salt, pepper, and parsley. Put the pieces of fish on this bed, sprinkle the surface of the fish with two tablespoons chopped butter, and add the wine, but avoid disturbing the butter. Cover the dish with foil and bake for fifteen minutes. When the fish is done, remove it from the sauce with a perforated spatula and keep it warm on the plate from which it will be served. Remove the dish with the sauce from the oven and heat it on top of the stove. Carefully add flour and water, which have been well mixed, and stir constantly. When well blended, raise the heat and thicken and reduce the sauce. Just before serving, and after you have removed the sauce from the heat, add the remaining three tablespoons of chopped butter to the sauce and pour over the fish.

To serve: Place quarters of lemons around the platter. This dish doesn't need a garnish, but boiled potatoes go well with any fish preparation; for this recipe, the small red ones, boiled and peeled, would be quite appropriate.

FILLET OF GRAY SOLE À LA CATALANE

I first made fillet of sole *à la Catalane* many years ago in Paris, using the readily available authentic sole from Normandy. Gray sole, with which Americans must do, is not a sole but a flounder, although it is of similar conformation and flavor.

If you are deft enough, you might offer this as the main dish of a not-too-large buffet—for ten or twelve people, for example. The fillets are served on a mild sauce made with fresh tomatoes; this dish requires no garnish.

INGREDIENTS FOR FIVE

2 lb fillets of gray sole (weight after being cleaned, boned, and skinned)

2 eggs, lightly beaten

1½ to 2 cups bread crumbs, not toasted

1½ Tbsp parsley, very finely chopped

salt and pepper

oil

butter

FOR THE SAUCE

1 medium onion, peeled and very finely chopped

3 large, ripe tomatoes, peeled, seeded, and chopped

1 Tbsp butter

1 Tbsp oil

1 clove garlic, mashed

salt and pepper

piece of bay leaf, the size of a dime

⅛ tsp leaf thyme

1 cup chicken or beef stock (or ½ cup stock and ½ cup dry white wine)

2 lemons, quartered and seeded

To make: Cut each fillet in two diagonally. Mix the
crumbs with the parsley, salt, and pepper. Dip each piece
of fillet in the beaten egg and then in the crumb mixture. Make sure that the layer of crumbs is even and
completely covers the fish; nothing looks less appetizing than a patchy job of breading. As each piece is
breaded, set it aside on a piece of waxed paper. Do not
allow the pieces to touch one another, and do not put
one on top of another. Put the fish in the refrigerator
while you make the sauce.

Prepare the sauce by sautéing, but not browning, the
onion and garlic in the oil and butter. When the onion
and garlic are soft, add the tomatoes and cook for ten
minutes. Then add the bay leaf, thyme, salt, pepper,
and stock (or stock and wine). Cook for twenty minutes. Mash the tomatoes in the sauce, but not too much;
the sauce should not be too smooth.

Set the oven at 150° (very low). Cover the bottom
of a large serving platter with the tomato sauce and
put the platter in the oven, but leave the door open.
Begin cooking the fish by heating butter and oil in
equal quantities in a large skillet or skillets. Use just
enough butter and oil to brown the fish crisply—about
one-eighth inch. Add more as required. Cook as many
pieces of fish at one time as you can without crowding
them, turning once. When done—a matter of minutes—
place the pieces on the tomato sauce. Serve with quartered lemons.

COURT BOUILLON

Poaching fish or any seafood means cooking over low
heat in a liquid. A court bouillon is a prepared liquid
designed to poach the fish and flavor it. It is prepared

(cooked in advance) because the flavorings include root vegetables, which impart flavor only after fairly lengthy cooking. Since a delicate fish must be cooked over low heat for a short time—from fifteen to twenty minutes—vegetables such as carrots, onions, and celery would contribute little if they were not cooked in the liquid in advance.

There are many different kinds of court bouillons, the simplest of which is salted water. The following recipe is one of the most flexible—excellent for both fresh and salt water fish, small or large, and also for crustaceans (shrimp, lobster, crab).

INGREDIENTS FOR ONE QUART

1 medium carrot, peeled and cut into thin slices

1 medium onion, thinly sliced

2 stalks celery (with some of the leaves), finely chopped

5 sprigs parsley (stems as well as leaves)

1 small bay leaf

$\frac{1}{6}$ tsp leaf thyme

juice of 1 medium lemon

2 cups dry white wine

2 cups water

To make: Put the above ingredients into a pot and cook until the vegetables are quite soft.

Note: If you have had a fish filleted and intend to poach the fillets, cook the fish head and bones in the court bouillon along with the other ingredients. This makes for a richer court bouillon.

FOWL

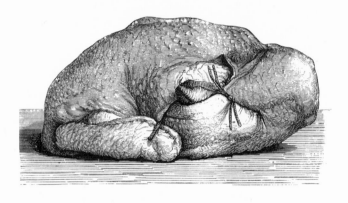

CHICKEN, turkey, and, to a degree, duck are staples of our diet; but I must say that because of the mediocre quality of a good deal of what is on the market, these items don't arouse much enthusiasm. When I was a boy, the only chickens we were familiar with were organically raised and freshly killed; and we certainly didn't take them for granted, although they were inexpensive and never in short supply. While I am quite aware that, given our immense urban population, we could not feed a nation such as ours by raising chickens or anything else by the old hit-or-miss methods of the local farmer, I still hold that chickens and turkeys ought to taste like chickens and turkeys, and

I believe this can be done. Just recently I have been buying freshly killed chickens raised in Maine which have the appearance and flavor of the French *Gatinais* chickens (after the chickens of Bresse, one of the most prized species of chicken in France), which indicates that somebody is doing something right.

As for ducks, I regret that the only type of duck generally available in the United States is the Long Island variety, with its thick layer of fat under the skin. It is most unsatisfactory, particularly since the duck must be cooked to death to get rid of that layer of fat. Ideally, the breast meat of duck should be served rare, which is impossible with the ducks available.

SAUTÉED CHICKEN WITH TARRAGON

Sautéed chicken with tarragon does not call for wine, truffles, or even mushrooms, but I think it is one of the better recipes for chicken breasts. And it is a quick dish to prepare. You may bone the breasts or have them boned, in which case they are ideal for buffet serving.

INGREDIENTS FOR FOUR

4 small chicken breasts (the entire breast), cut in half lengthwise

flour

1 Tbsp dried tarragon

2½ cups beef stock

⅛ tsp cayenne pepper

juice of ½ medium lemon

olive or peanut oil

[99]

To make: Wipe the chicken with a damp cloth and remove and reject all fat. Dredge the breasts in flour, making sure that all the surfaces are covered. Shake off excess flour and set the chicken pieces aside. Simmer the beef stock, tarragon, cayenne pepper, and lemon juice in a pot while you cook the chicken. Pour one-half inch of oil in a skillet and heat until almost smoking. Add the chicken (three or four pieces at a time; they should not be crowded) and brown well, especially on the skin side. Raise and lower the heat as required; the chicken should brown, but not burn. When each batch is sufficiently browned, remove from the pan and set aside. When all the pieces are browned and set aside, pour off all the oil from the pan, leaving the brown bits on the bottom and the slight amount of oil adhering to the pan. Return the chicken to the pan and pour the stock over it through a sieve. Cover the skillet with a lid, if it has one, or seal with aluminum foil. Cook over the very lowest heat until tender, but avoid overcooking. It should not take more than twenty minutes, but to be sure, test with a fork. Just before serving, remove the chicken pieces from the skillet and place them on a heated platter, skin-side up. Remove as much fat as possible from the cooking liquid and then rapidly reduce it, scraping the bottom of the pan to pick up all the brown bits. This must be cooked over very high heat long enough to produce a smooth, lightly thickened sauce that will just coat the meat.

Note: Adding one teaspoon of tomato paste livens the color of the sauce without altering its flavor.

To serve: Serve with mashed, baked, or sautéed potatoes, green beans with basil, and baked or grilled tomatoes (see p. 187), preferably small ones.

POULET CELESTINE

Poulet Celestine, a sautéed chicken dish, is a particularly good example of how the French handle tomatoes (see p. 267). The following Lyonnaise recipe is that of the chef Rousselot.

INGREDIENTS FOR TWO OR THREE

1 young fine chicken, cut up as for a fricassee

butter

1 cup mushrooms, sliced

1 medium tomato, peeled, seeded, and chopped

⅔ cup dry white wine

½ cup jus de viande (see basic stock on p. 19)

1 Tbsp fine cognac

salt

¼ tsp poivre doux d'Espagne (If you cannot find this, substitute fine Hungarian paprika.)

1 Tbsp parsley, very finely chopped

1 clove garlic, very, very finely chopped

To make: Sauté the chicken in butter until the pieces are golden brown; add the mushrooms and tomato. Cook for five minutes and add the wine, *jus de viande,* cognac, salt, and *poivre doux d'Espagne.* Continue to cook for fifteen minutes, and remove the pieces of meat to a heated platter. Remove the fat from the sauce, and add the parsley and garlic. If the sauce is too thin, reduce it over high heat and continue cooking until it thickens.

[1 0 1]

To serve: Pour the sauce over the meat and serve. This dish doesn't really need a garnish, as good bread supports it very well. If you like, however, serve sautéed potatoes (see p. 201); they won't hurt the dish.

POACHED CHICKEN

This method of poaching chicken is foolproof and little trouble. The result is invariably juicy, tasty, and *intact* —especially important if you want to serve a whole cold chicken. But even if you intend to serve it sliced or chopped, you will find the meat juicy and not stringy.

INGREDIENTS FOR THREE TO FOUR

3½ lb chicken

chicken giblets, excluding the liver

3 stalks celery (with a few leaves), finely chopped

3 medium carrots, finely chopped

*1 bunch scallions or 1 medium onion, chopped
(If you have the scallions, retain ⅓ of the green part.)*

1 large or 2 medium leeks (only the white part), chopped

1 medium parsnip, peeled and chopped (optional)

handful of parsley (leaves and stems), roughly chopped

salt and pepper

To make: Put all the ingredients except the chicken into a large pot. Add sufficient water to cover, and prepare a court bouillon. Wash the chicken well and truss it securely. Add the chicken to the pot with enough water to cover it. Bring the liquid slowly to a boil, then turn the heat down to very low. Skim the surface of the liquid carefully, moving the chicken about by tilting the pot. After the stock is clear, turn up the heat again and when it is just at the boil, turn it off completely. Cover the pot tightly with a close-fitting lid, put a weight on it, and forget it until completely cooled. Because the cooling takes several hours, this dish is best prepared the night before serving.

Note: Obviously, the bouillon from chicken cooked this way won't be very rich; the method, after all, is designed to keep the richness in the chicken. If you want richer soup, add a pound or more of chicken wings or backs and simmer them for an hour.

ROAST CHICKEN OR CAPON

A chicken of first quality, properly roasted, is an elegant dish. But first-quality chickens are hard to find, and they are rarely properly roasted. A first-quality chicken should be freshly killed, not frozen, although quick-frozen chickens are far superior to cold storage chickens, which have little flavor. Even worse, cold storage chickens often have too much of the wrong flavor, due, no doubt, to what they subsisted on when alive—I suspect fortified shredded newspapers, reinforced with fish debris and chemicals. Having the chicken freshly killed is not enough. The chicken has to be fine to begin with, which depends on the raiser and what he feeds his chickens. In other words, if you want to serve first-class roast chicken, search out a butcher who sells freshly killed chickens of the best quality. When you find him, you may be startled by his prices; but after you have tasted the bird, you will realize that there is as much difference between such a chicken and one from the supermarket as there is between a prime porterhouse steak and a piece of chuck.

INGREDIENTS FOR FOUR

1 5- or 6-lb capon (One pound of chicken is usually allowed per person, when serving en famille, but for guests it is nicer to have a larger chicken to allow for preference. It makes carving easier and if you have any left over, so much the better; cold roast chicken is very good.)

⅛ lb butter

salt and pepper

ONE OF THE FOLLOWING FOR SEASONING

3 sprigs parsley (leaves and stems)

⅛ lb butter

6 shallots or scallions, peeled

salt and pepper

1 Tbsp dried tarragon

6 scallions

2 sprigs parsley

⅛ lb butter

salt and pepper

1 lemon, peeled and sliced

3 sprigs parsley

1 medium onion

⅛ lb butter

salt and pepper

To make: Allow one-eighth pound butter to soften and, with a piece of paper towel, spread it over the skin of the chicken. Sprinkle the chicken with salt and pepper. Place one of the above seasoning mixtures in the cavity of the chicken.

The chicken, while roasting, should not touch the bottom of the pan, or it will swim in its own fat and very likely burn. If you don't have a pan with a grill insert, use any grill you have handy. If necessary, place the grill on top and over the edges of a high-sided pan, taking care that the chicken does not extend over the sides of the pan.

Preheat your oven to 350°. Roast the chicken for two hours if six pounds, for one hour and forty minutes if five pounds. After one hour baste or brush the bird with the fat from the pan, and continue basting every fifteen minutes until the chicken is done. Do not baste with anything but the pan juices and do not add any liquid. Liquid makes steam and, in effect, introduces a braising element.

The most effective way of determining if the chicken is done is to plunge a two-pronged fork into the thickest part of the leg: if the juice that flows is clear, the chicken is done; if it is even faintly pink, cook the chicken ten minutes longer and test again.

When the chicken is done, turn the oven down to 125°, put the chicken on a platter and put the platter on the open door of the oven, turning the platter around from time to time. The chicken should rest for twenty minutes so that the flesh will firm and the juices will be fixed in the meat. If you like, make an improvised warming oven with aluminum foil as described on p. 275.

INGREDIENTS FOR THE SAUCE

chicken giblets, excluding the liver

2 cups chicken stock or 2 chicken bouillon cubes dissolved in water

1 medium onion

1 stalk celery (with some leaves)

3 sprigs parsley

1 medium carrot

½ cup dry white wine

salt and pepper

chicken pan juices

To make: It is best to make the sauce in advance, but you don't have to. Use the giblets, excluding the liver which has too pronounced a flavor. (Don't waste the liver though. Set it aside and, when you have time, sauté it in butter until firm but still pink inside. Allow it to cool. Serve it sliced in a salad to follow the chicken course.)

Cook the neck, gizzard, and heart in chicken stock or in plain water with two chicken bouillon cubes. Add the onion, celery, parsley, carrot, wine, salt, and pepper. Cook for two hours over low heat, adding more water as it reduces. (If you want to serve the gizzard and the heart, remove them from the stock when they are tender, chop very fine, and set aside.) When the stock is done, strain it, remove the surface fat, and over high heat reduce it by one-third. This completes the first step in making the sauce.

The second step begins when the chicken is removed to a platter and the juices in its cavity have been poured into the roasting pan. Remove most of the fat from the pan, but be careful to leave any meat juices as well as the brown bits on the bottom of the pan. Put the roasting pan on one of the burners on top of the stove, add the stock, and over high heat, scraping and mixing, blend the stock with the pan juices. Just before serving, pour a few spoonsful of the sauce over the chicken and serve the rest, to which you have added the chopped gizzard and heart, in a sauce-boat.

To serve: The ideal accompaniment to roast chicken is mashed potatoes, but, heaven forbid, not the packaged variety. Mash the potatoes with milk, butter, and sour cream. Admittedly, the combination of mashed potatoes and roast chicken is not very French; in fact, it is very American, but I'll stick to my guns about its appropriateness. If you want to make a grander presentation, serve the chicken with artichoke hearts filled with little peas, *pommes Anna,* and grilled tomatoes, or any combination that pleases you. I like cranberries with roast chicken, which is also distinctly non-French, for their tartness is said to impinge on the flavor of wine. As a matter of fact, this is correct, but the French eat a good many things with wine that are quite as tart as cranberries (for example, *cornichons* with boiled beef or with pâté and many hors d'oeuvre with vinaigrette sauce—items that I have seen countless French-

men consume and never without wine). To complete
the garnish, I suggest creamed poached scallions and
green beans with basil.

CHICKEN BREASTS WITH MADEIRA WINE
AND LIME JUICE

Of all the foolproof recipes I know, roast chicken
breasts with Madeira wine and lime juice takes first
prize. It is elegant and simple to serve.

INGREDIENTS FOR FOUR

4 small chicken breasts (a whole breast per person)

4 Tbsp olive oil

juice of 1 lime

2 Tbsp dried tarragon

¾ cup beef stock

⅓ cup dry Madeira wine

⅛ tsp cayenne pepper

salt

lemons, quartered

To make: Preheat the oven to 350°. Brush the chicken
breasts on both sides with olive oil. Place them, skin-
side up, in a pan or on doubled heavy aluminum foil
and cook in the oven for one hour. While the breasts
are cooking, add the tarragon to the beef stock and
simmer for twenty minutes. Strain the stock, add the
lime juice, Madeira wine, cayenne pepper, and salt
and keep warm. After cooking for one hour, take the
chicken from the oven and pour off all the fat in the

pan. Return to the oven and cook for thirty minutes more, basting frequently with the stock and wine mixture. Keep adding the mixture until it is all used up, brushing or basting the chicken breasts frequently. If, after one hour and fifteen minutes of total cooking, the chicken breasts are not browning well, raise the heat very high. The cooked chicken should be a nice mahogany color, and the basting liquid should be almost completely absorbed. In any case, no sauce is necessary for this dish.

To serve: Garnish the platter with quartered lemons with the seeds removed. Serve with canned shoestring potatoes and watercress. Heat the potatoes in their cans for five minutes in the oven, but don't forget to open one end of each can. These potatoes burn very easily. Season the watercress with lemon juice, salt, and pepper.

Note: A nice variation is to baste the chicken—after pouring off all the fat after the first hour of baking— with Chinese plum sauce, if you can find it, or with apricot jelly or preserves into which you have mixed one small grated onion, a pinch of cayenne pepper, and a little soy sauce. Serve with rice combined with finely chopped, sautéed snow peas. Have chutney, hot mustard, and soy sauce available on the table.

TURKEY

Despite a few dissenting opinions, it is generally recognized that the turkey is indigenous only to the North American continent. It is thus, far more than any other meat, distinctly American; and while I don't think chauvinism has a place in any cuisine, I do feel we could be a little more imaginative in the treatment of our national bird.

There was a time not so long ago when turkeys were available only during the periods of two holidays—Thanksgiving and Christmas—and everyone enjoyed their relative novelty. Those days are gone, and turkeys are now available all year round. But in view of a prolonged steak bender on the part of Americans and the high cost of fillet of beef—a day's pay—turkey has become a poor relation. This state of affairs indicates a lack of culinary judgment and invention.

A plea for more imaginative treatment of turkey would not have much point if there were something essentially limiting about the bird itself. That is not the case. The French have created masterpieces with turkey and Brillat-Savarin, in *The Physiology of Taste*, has termed it *un des plus beaux cadeaux que le Nouveau Monde ait fait à l'Ancien* ("one of the finest gifts the New World has given to the Old World"). A contemporary estimate of how the French regard turkey may be found in the pages of Simon Arbellot's book, *Un Gastronome se Penche sur son Passe*—a most entertaining account of the author's experiences and adventures in Paris and elsewhere as a writer, critic, and professional gastronome. This diverting and informative book includes a select handful of recipes, one of which is for *dinde en daube* (braised turkey) as prepared in Périgord, a region of France rich in truffles and *foie gras* and noted for its good food. The *daube* (stew) does not, however, include truffles or *foie gras*; the turkey stands on its own. (The recipe for braised turkey that follows is identical with *dinde en daube*, the only modification being the substitution of bourbon whiskey for cognac.)

Turkey and truffles make a perfect combination. But I

will give one overrefined recipe, which combines both *foie gras* and truffles with turkey, only as a curiosity. Although it dates from another epoch, the recipe indicates strikingly something of the regard the French have for turkey. It establishes its tone right at the beginning with the direction to fill the turkey with truffles five days before it is to be cooked. Then, on the day you cook the bird—and here is the part I like—you remove the truffles and throw them away. You then start with a new batch of truffles, inserting truffle slices seasoned with cognac under the skin of the turkey and filling the turkey's cavity with a mixture of truffles and fresh *foie gras*. The final direction, startlingly sober in its context, is to put the turkey on a spit and cook it until done.

The following recipes for turkey, each eminently practical, include a variety of stuffings. However, don't look here for the singular, bread-loaded, papier-mâché-flavored stuffing encountered in certain restaurants. That recipe is a secret—and I hope it remains one.

ROAST TURKEY

The first requirement for producing a first-class roast turkey is to obtain a freshly killed bird, easily done in cities and towns and not impossible in many small towns. Above all, avoid cold storage turkeys; fresh-frozen are far better. I am obstinate, however, about using nothing but the best when undertaking something as large as a fourteen-pound turkey; and if you know what you are buying, the result is predictable: a succulent, tasty bird or a dry, uninteresting one.

INGREDIENTS FOR TEN

1 freshly killed 14-lb turkey

1 lemon

2 Tbsp butter

salt and pepper

FOR THE GRAVY

gizzard, heart and neck of turkey (I don't use the turkey liver. I find its flavor too strong for its importance. The French do something nice with it. They sauté it in butter until just done—firm and pink. It is chilled, sliced, and added to a lettuce salad with a sliced hard boiled egg.)

1 medium onion

1 carrot, chopped

2 or 3 stalks celery (with leaves)

parsley sprigs

salt and pepper

To make: Preheat the oven to 350°. Singe the turkey carefully on all sides, but just enough to burn off any fuzz or incipient feathers. Wipe the bird well, and truss it by tying the wings close to the body and the legs in such a way that the cavity is closed. Melt the butter and spread it over the turkey with a paper towel. Dust the entire surface of the turkey with salt and pepper, place it breast up on a grill in a *low-sided* roasting pan, and place it in the oven. Cook it for from five to five and one-half hours, basting frequently during the last ninety minutes. There are several ways of determining if the turkey is done:

Take the end of the leg bone and move it to and fro. If it moves easily, the turkey is done. If it is resistant, further cooking is required.

Plunge a fork into the thigh joint. If the liquid that flows is perfectly clear and without a trace of pink, the turkey is done; otherwise, continue cooking for fifteen minutes or more.

The professional method is to check the liquid in the cavity by tilting the turkey. Again, if there is a trace of pink, it is not done. If the juices are clear, the bird is ready to be removed.

When the turkey has been removed from the oven and placed on a platter, it must be allowed to rest in a warm place for twenty-five minutes before carving (see p. 275 for an improvised warming oven). If this procedure is followed, the juice will remain in the turkey where it belongs.

To make the gravy: Put the gizzard, heart, neck, onion, carrot, celery, parsley, and salt and pepper in a pot, add water to cover, and bring the mixture to a boil. Reduce heat, skim the broth carefully, and cook until the gizzard is quite tender. Remove the giblets to a dish and cover with cellophane wrap. Continue cooking the giblet broth until somewhat reduced, strain, and remove and reject the fat. Set aside and keep warm. When the turkey has been removed from the oven and put on a platter, pour off all the fat from the roasting pan, being careful to retain any meat juice under the fat, as well as the brown parts adhering to the pan. Put the roasting pan over a burner on top of the stove, turn

---

the heat up to high, pour in some of the giblet stock, and, carefully scraping, blend the liquid until smooth. Pour this into a serving dish with the giblets. This is the gravy, and it doesn't need thickening, although there is no law against it.

STUFFED TURKEY

Except for different instructions in handling the giblets and the factor that a stuffed bird must be cooked longer (five minutes more per pound), the turkey is cooked precisely as is an unstuffed turkey (see above). Following is a selection of stuffing choices.

Note: Never stuff a turkey more than a few hours in advance; and, above all, do not stuff a turkey and put it in the refrigerator overnight. To do so is to run the risk of food poisoning.

BASIC STUFFING

I made the first version of this stuffing years ago after some preparatory experimenting, spurred on by the need to devise a stuffing that avoided both the common pork-sausage base and, at the other extreme, the prohibitively expensive truffle and *foie gras* base of the great classical recipes. Eventually I developed what I consider a basic recipe that can stand on its own or incorporate chestnuts, oysters, chicken breast meat, veal, or ham—singly or in combinations. I have even used it, somewhat modified, for stuffing lamb (spinach added), veal (Canadian bacon added), and fish (less celery, but more mushrooms added).

INGREDIENTS FOR AN EIGHT-POUND TURKEY

1 large bunch celery (rejecting the outer stalks and most of the leaves), very finely chopped

2 bunches scallions (with some of the green parts), finely chopped

1 lb mushrooms, very finely chopped (The mushrooms should be very white and unopened. Do not wash; clean by rubbing them in a towel. Reject only the dark stem ends.)

2 Tbsp parsley, very finely chopped

2 egg yolks, lightly beaten

2 cups dried white bread crumbs

1/4 lb butter, half of it chopped

1/2 cup heavy cream

salt and pepper, to taste

turkey bouillon (Make in advance by cooking the gizzard, neck, and heart in water with a few of the outer celery stalks, a few celery leaves, a chopped carrot, a medium onion, several sprigs of parsley, salt, and pepper. Cook for at least one hour.)

Note: If you like the flavor of turkey liver, sauté it in butter until firm, but still pink inside. Mash it with a fork and mix it into the stuffing. Personally, I find the flavor of turkey liver too strong and pervasive for its importance, but I do like it sautéed, chilled, and sliced in a lettuce salad.

To make: In a large pan with a cover, heat one-eighth pound butter. Add the scallions and celery and cook, covered, until the celery is tender. This takes at least thirty minutes; crisp celery in stuffing tastes somewhat

[1 1 5]

like destroyed chop suey. Add the mushrooms and cook for ten minutes more, uncovered. Allow the mixture to cool. Then put it in a large bowl and add the parsley, egg yolks, one-eighth pound chopped butter, salt, and pepper. Mix well, adding one cup of the bread crumbs. Add the cream; mix again, adding the other cup of bread crumbs. Now, and carefully, add turkey bouillon until the mixture is thoroughly moist, but not sodden. But it is better to use too much bouillon than not enough; a too-dry stuffing produces a sort of rubbery cake.

To prepare the turkey, stuff both the body and neck cavities, but do not force stuffing into the bird; stuffing expands as it cooks. If you have some left over, cook it in a pyrex dish for one hour and twenty minutes in the oven with the turkey. In fact, all of these stuffing recipes may be cooked separately, which is advisable if you cook your turkey on a spit or rotisserie.

Variations on the basic stuffing can include many tempting combinations.

WITH OYSTERS

Use two-thirds the amount of celery and mushrooms given in the basic recipe. Add an additional one-half cup of bread crumbs and one pint of oysters with their liquid. Given the oyster liquid, it is necessary to reduce the amount of bouillon used to moisten the dressing.

WITH CHESTNUTS

Use the same basic recipe, but omit the mushrooms. Boil one pound of chestnuts for ten minutes. Drain the chestnuts and remove the shells and inner skins, working as quickly as possible; when cool, the shells and skins are very difficult to remove. Put the chestnuts back in the pot, cover with salted water, and cook for thirty minutes or until a chestnut will crumble easily. When done, drain the chestnuts, break into pieces, and mix into the stuffing. An ounce or two of mild cooked ham, finely chopped, may be added.

WITH HAM

Into the basic stuffing, mix one-half pound of very thinly sliced, mild boiled ham, cut in thin strips.

WITH GROUND VEAL

Use one-half the given quantity of celery and mushrooms. Sauté one pound of very finely ground lean veal in butter until it changes color. Mix it into the stuffing with one-half cup of not-too-dry white wine. The white wine replaces the same quantity of bouillon.

WITH HERBS

Marinate one tablespoon dried tarragon and two tablespoons very finely chopped parsley in one-half cup of white wine for one hour. Mix it into the stuffing, wine and all. Use less bouillon to moisten the stuffing.

WITH THE TURKEY GIBLETS

When the turkey bouillon is cooked, remove the giblets (gizzard, heart, and neck) and allow them to cool. Remove as much meat from the neck as possible and chop it. Also chop the heart and the edible parts of the gizzard. Add them to the stuffing mixture. If you like the flavor of liver in the stuffing, sauté the turkey liver in a little butter, mash it with a fork, and mix with the other giblets into the stuffing.

WITH POACHED CHICKEN BREAST

This, to me, is the best of the variations; the chicken in the stuffing tastes like super-fine turkey and the texture is superb. There is very little to making it. Add the meat of one medium chicken breast, poached, boned, and skinned. Chop the meat and mix it lightly into the stuffing. If you like tarragon, flavor the turkey broth with one tablespoon and strain it before mixing. Adding the chicken breast without reducing the quantities of the other ingredients will give you more stuffing, of course, but don't worry about leftovers.

RICE STUFFING FOR TURKEY

This rice stuffing of Mediterranean origin is hardly in the American tradition, but, in a way I can't define, it's festive.

INGREDIENTS FOR A NINE-POUND TURKEY

5½ cups rice, cooked in turkey stock (Make the stock by cooking the neck, gizzard, and heart of the turkey in water with 2 stalks of celery, a few celery leaves, 2 carrots, a medium yellow onion, a few sprigs of parsley, salt, and pepper. Cook until the gizzard is tender.)

½ cup currants, marinated in white wine for one hour

giblets (used to make the stock), chopped

4 Tbsp pine nuts (pignoli)

2 Tbsp parsley, chopped

2 hard-boiled egg yolks, finely chopped

[1 1 8]

To make: If you use rice that needs washing, wash it until there is no trace of starch on the surface of the water. Cook it until it is almost done, but not quite. If the rice is at all sticky, add two or three tablespoons of melted butter and mix lightly. When the rice has thoroughly cooled, add all the other ingredients and mix lightly, but well.

POACHED BREAST OF TURKEY

Have you heard complaints that the white meat of turkey is too dry? This may be true of an improperly roasted turkey, but it does not apply to turkey breast, slowly poached and flavored with vegetables and herbs. Prepared this way, the meat is firm but juicy, and very easy to slice and serve—cold or hot—in aspic, salads, or a sauce.

INGREDIENTS FOR EIGHT

breast of a medium (8- to 9-lb) turkey

4 stalks celery (with half the leaves), finely chopped

2 bunches scallions (with half the green parts), finely chopped

2 medium carrots, scraped and finely chopped

1 small parsnip, finely chopped (optional)

3 Tbsp parsley, finely chopped

salt and pepper

To make: Put the turkey breast into a large, thick-bottomed pot. Cover it well with cold water, bring it slowly to a boil, turn down the heat immediately, and

[1 1 9]

skim. Continue skimming until the liquid is quite clear. Add all the other ingredients and cover the pot. Turn down the heat to very low and cook for one hour and forty-five minutes. If you intend to serve the breast cold, let it cool in the broth. Whether you serve it hot or cold, remove and reject the skin.

To serve: Here are a few samples of what can be done with a poached turkey breast:

Slice it and serve cold with chopped aspic made from the turkey broth.

Slice it, cut into strips, and serve cold in a salad.

Slice it and serve with a sauce made of the turkey stock, Madeira wine, and mushrooms. Sauté the mushrooms separately and add to the sauce five minutes before serving. Serve on toast with a garnish of asparagus.

Slice and serve in a cream sauce on rice.

Slice and serve in a dark sauce made from the turkey stock, with sweet potatoes, stuffing cooked separately (see p. 114), and cranberries.

BRAISED TURKEY

Braised turkey is traditionally served for supper after midnight mass in Perigord, but various versions of it, sometimes called *daube* or *étouffade* are popular throughout the Southwest of France. When properly cooked, it certainly takes care of the most common complaint about turkey—its dryness.

INGREDIENTS FOR SEVEN

1 9-lb. turkey, cut up as for frying

2 medium carrots, roughly chopped

2 medium onions, roughly chopped

2 stalks celery with some of the leaves, roughly chopped

1 bay leaf

½ tsp dried leaf thyme

3 parsley sprigs, leaves and stems

2 jiggers whiskey

2 cups dry white wine

salt and pepper

3 Tbsp butter

3 Tbsp olive oil

water

1 lb fresh mushrooms (optional)

To make: Melt the butter in a large dutch oven (preferably enameled cast iron with a heavy cover), add the olive oil, and brown the turkey pieces, three or four at a time, over medium heat. As the pieces brown, remove them to a dish. When all the pieces are browned and set aside, add the carrots, celery, onions, bay leaf, thyme, and parsley to the dutch oven, and brown them well in the same fat, stirring frequently. Then add the whiskey; and, when it is heated somewhat, ignite the alcohol fumes, tilting the dutch oven to and fro to make sure the whiskey is thoroughly ignited.

Put the turkey pieces (white meat on top) on the vegetables, add salt and pepper, the white wine, and sufficient water to barely cover the turkey pieces. Cover the dutch oven and cook over very low heat for two hours or until done. Begin testing with a fork after one hour and thirty minutes. When the meat is just done, remove the pieces to a warm platter, strain the sauce into a dish, and remove and reject all the fat from the sauce. If you intend to serve from the dutch oven, wash it and return the meat and the sauce to it. If you wish—they go well with turkey—trim and peel one pound of mushrooms. Sauté them in a little butter and a few drops of lemon juice. Cook them for about seven minutes over medium heat, and add them to the turkey.

In my opinion, the sauce of braised turkey does not need thickening, but if you prefer you may thicken it by blending two tablespoons of melted butter with four tablespoons of flour. Continue cooking until the mixture browns, stirring constantly. Then, a little at a time, add some of the turkey sauce, stirring constantly until the mixture is very smooth. Strain it over the braised turkey, tilting the dutch oven in all directions to coat all the pieces thoroughly.

To serve: Serve with boiled potatoes sprinkled with parsley, and grilled tomatoes (see p. 187).

BEEF

BEEF is certainly the most popular meat in the United States. In fact, if all the restaurants, pubs, and clubs that feature prime ribs of beef were laid end to end, they would probably traverse the continent. There is, however, absolutely nothing to producing a superb standing rib roast except for one very important step that has nothing to do with the cooking: selecting a fine piece of meat. The rub is that, as in Paris, London, Vienna, Rome, and Madrid, the restaurants get the best of it. The problem is not merely a matter of selecting by grade—prime or choice. I know a very fine butcher on New York's Upper East Side who ages his meat thoroughly; and a look around his refrigerators gives me something of the sort of sensation a miser must feel at the sight of a vault full of money. He chooses his sides of beef according to his own criteria; prime and choice grades are well mixed. This sort of buying is possible for a professional equipped with a singleness of purpose and years of experience. I advise you—especially if you have a standing rib roast in mind—to find the best butcher around. But be prepared for high prices. I can assure you that the restaurants, pubs, and clubs do not get their meat for nothing.

STEAK SANDWICH

A steak sandwich has come to mean everything from a large steak flanked by a couple of miniscule pieces of toast to a few slices of flank steak, or some other version of London broil, served on a hamburger bun. The latter is notable as a sort of reverse accomplishment—pairing the worst of beef with the worst of bread. The sandwich I am dealing with here is quite another matter; it combines the best of beef with the best of bread and is very definitely a sandwich.

INGREDIENTS FOR TEN

4 lb sirloin or porterhouse steak (weight after all fat, sinews, and gristle have been removed), cut into thin slices and lightly pounded

crisp French or Italian bread or hero rolls of the very best quality

butter

salt and pepper

[**1 2 4**]

To make: Because these sandwiches should be served immediately and only three or, at the most, four can be made at a time, it is wise to enlist someone to do the rushing. Heat a tablespoon of butter in a large, heavy-bottomed skillet—or use two skillets. When the butter is just beginning to brown, add as many pieces of the steak as the pan or pans will accommodate without crowding. Working rapidly, brown the slices on both sides, turning once. In the meantime have your assistant heat the bread in the oven. Split one or two lengthy sections of bread or whole hero rolls lengthwise, quickly butter the bottom half of each section, and add the steak, salt, and pepper. Put on the top piece of bread, press firmly, and send it off. Start on the next batch, and so on. (As the pan juices accumulate, soak them up with the top pieces of bread. Add fresh butter for each batch.)

Steak cooked this way, although in a larger format, is served in some restaurants under the name *Steak Diane.* Since it produces the maximum amount of surface, this method also produces the most flavor.

To serve: These sandwiches need nothing in the way of condiments, except possibly chopped scallions, but that is a matter of taste. Serve red wine and beer and, if you wish, pass or have at hand olives, cherry tomatoes, scallions, and potato chips.

Note: As a variation, using the same method try very thinly sliced, boned pork loin. Nowadays, good pork is harder to find than good beef, so take advantage of it if you run onto some. The cut should be small, not clammy, smooth textured, and, above all, light in color. Red pork and red veal have become accepted anomalies.

Another variation is veal with peppers. Here, in particular, the veal should be white and dry. Grill the peppers, remove the skins, cut into strips, and keep warm in the oven with the bread. A dash of lemon juice on the peppers doesn't hurt.

HALF-MINUTE STEAKS

Half-minute steaks are an excellent lunch or supper dish, easily and quickly made. I advise you to slice the meat yourself. Butchers won't do it with the necessary neatness, and, if you want to learn something about meat-cutting, you may as well start with this.

INGREDIENTS FOR SIX

3 lb fillet of beef or 5 lb sirloin, shell, or porterhouse steak (Remove bones if other steak than the fillet is being used, all fat, and nerves. Slice the beef thin, cutting against the grain. The result will be an assortment of sizes and shapes, but that is of no importance; the objective is to achieve slices of uniform thickness, about one-eighth inch thick. Put the slices between two pieces of waxed paper and flatten them with a heavy skillet, but do not pound. Set them aside until ready to be used.)

3 Tbsp butter

1 cup strong beef stock

½ cup dry Madeira wine

1 small can black truffles (with juice), sliced

1 Tbsp lemon juice

1 tsp parsley, very finely chopped

⅛ tsp cayenne pepper

salt and black pepper, freshly ground

To make: Melt two tablespoons of butter in a large, shallow skillet over high heat. When the butter begins to smoke, add meat slices, allowing some room between the pieces. Turn each slice once. You will have to cook the meat in several batches. Remove cooked pieces to a warm platter, add a little more butter to the skillet, and continue until all the meat is done. When all the meat is set aside on a warm dish, add the beef stock, Madeira wine, salt, and pepper to the pan and cook over highest heat until the volume is reduced by half. Remove from heat, add the lemon juice, cayenne pepper, chopped parsley, and the canned truffle (or truffles) with its juice. Mix in about one tablespoon or more of butter cut in small pieces, stir until it melts, and pour the sauce over the meat.

To serve: Serve the steak on round croutons of white bread with the crust removed, fried in butter on both sides. Garnish with shoestring potatoes and watercress, seasoned with salt, pepper, and a sprinkle of lemon juice. Canned shoestring potatoes are excellent and merely require heating in the oven, but, again, don't forget to open one end of the can.

Note: If preferred, mushrooms may be used instead of truffles. Slice and sauté one-half pound of mushrooms separately in butter and lemon juice, and add them to the sauce just before pouring it over the meat.

GRILLED RIBS OF BEEF

A standing rib roast is a fine thing, but often when I have a small roast (consisting, say, of the first two or three ribs) I cut it into two or three thick slices, with a rib bone to each slice, and cook the slices under the broiler. This method takes much less time than roasting; there is more brown surface and, to my taste, more flavor. Carving the meat is also easier, since it is not sliced against the grain of the meat, but against the rib bone in large pieces, as with a steak.

INGREDIENTS FOR FIVE TO SEVEN

5½- to 6-lb roast of beef (rib), preferably the first two ribs (Trim off and reject most of the fat. Cut the meat between the rib bones into two pieces —or have your butcher do it for you.)

salt and pepper

oil

pinch of rosemary, freshly ground (optional)

1 or 2 cloves garlic (optional)

To make: Other than salt and pepper, the meat doesn't need seasoning, but if you like garlic, rub a clove or two over the surface of the meat before brushing it with oil and broiling. A nice touch is to sprinkle the roast—after brushing it with oil—with rosemary, freshly ground in a pepper grinder. But use very little; rosemary in any quantity tends to take over. Put the meat slices on a grill (to raise them from the pan) and under the broiler. Turn them as often as necessary.

To serve: Allow the grilled ribs to rest for a few minutes before putting them on the table. The accompaniments are French-fried or baked potatoes, grilled tomatoes, and watercress.

Note: If you like a sauce with the meat, add one-fourth cup dry Madeira wine to one cup of basic sauce (see

p. 19) and heat it. Just before serving, add the juice of one-fourth lemon and a pinch of cayenne pepper. If you feel extravagant, add one small can of black truffles, chopped. If you do not have basic sauce at hand, or do not wish to go to the trouble of making it, use a can of beef broth, reduce it by one-third, add the Madeira, and continue as above. Do not use what is known as canned beef gravy—a substance that might go well with a braised newspaper, but certainly has nothing whatever to do with good beef.

HAMBURGER ROLLS

As I have noted elsewhere, shape influences flavor, and this recipe is a good instance. In general, hamburger tends to be hamburger, whether it is called Salisbury steak, chopped sirloin, or burger on a bun. These hamburger rolls are something a bit different.

INGREDIENTS FOR SIX

2 lb round steak, ground with its fat

salt and pepper

½ cup beef stock

1 tsp lemon juice

¼ cup dry Madeira wine or a not-too-dry white wine

1 Tbsp butter

To make: Using a quantity of ground beef comparable to the bulk of a large egg, with your hands form tapered, flattened ovals. This should make from nine to ten rolls to one pound of beef. Mold the ovals loosely but firmly; if you press them too much, they will crack during the cooking. Sauté them in butter or in a mixture of butter and oil, pouring off the fat from the pan as it accumulates. Do not use high heat. Make a pan gravy by adding the beef stock, lemon juice, and wine. Place the meat rolls on a hot platter and reduce the mixture in the pan over very high heat. Scrape up all the brown bits in the pan and add salt and pepper. Just before pouring the sauce over the meat, add the butter, cut into small pieces.

To serve: Serve with mashed potatoes and a lettuce salad.

BRAISED SHORT RIBS OF BEEF

Of the many cuts of beef, the short rib is perhaps the most succulent. Auguste Escoffier, who was certainly one of the greatest chefs, wrote about the short rib: "Boiled, surrounded by the vegetables that were cooked with it, and accompanied by a creamed horseradish sauce, it merits the honor of a royal table."

Short ribs contain a good deal of fat, which keeps them juicy, but, because of the fat and the bone, they are not as economical as they might seem. In any case, select the leanest, meatiest short ribs available and count on at least one pound per person.

INGREDIENTS FOR SIX

6 lb short ribs of beef

4 Tbsp oil

2 large onions, peeled and roughly chopped

2 medium carrots, peeled and quartered

2 stalks celery (with some of the leaves), cut in large pieces

2 medium bay leaves

¼ tsp leaf thyme

4 sprigs parsley (stems as well as leaves)

salt and pepper

2 ounces dried mushrooms, preferably Polish, or ¾ lb fresh mushrooms (optional, but desirable)

2 cups red Burgundy wine (optional, but desirable)

2 jiggers whiskey (optional, but desirable)

To make: Preheat the oven to 325°. Heat the oil in an enameled cast-iron Dutch oven with a heavy cover or any large, thick-bottomed pot with a tight-fitting cover. Add the ribs, two or three at a time, and brown each piece thoroughly on all sides. This means really browning—a process which, if done right, assures the rich, dark gravy characteristic of this dish. Don't crowd the pot during the browning; if you do, moisture from the meat will produce steam which will effectively stop the browning process. As each piece is browned, remove it to a large plate. Continue until all the pieces are browned and set aside on the plate. Then add to the pan the onions, carrots, celery, salt, and pepper. Brown the vegetables well, stirring frequently. Lower the heat and add the bay leaves, thyme, and parsley. Cook for five minutes, stirring from time to time. (If you have decided to use the two jiggers of whiskey, add them at this point. Raise the heat under the Dutch oven, tilt the pan in all directions, and light the fumes of the alcohol. Continue tilting the vessel until the flame dies out.) Now put the pieces of meat into the Dutch oven, fitting them in as evenly as possible, in one or two layers depending on the size of the Dutch oven. Add enough water so that it comes up to two-thirds of the height of the meat. (If you intend to use the wine, add it now, which means two less cups of water.) Put the cover on the Dutch oven and put it in the 325° oven. Cook for from slightly over two hours to slightly over three hours, depending on the quality of the meat. Test the short ribs with a fork after two hours, but, if you have any doubt, cut off a piece of lean meat and test it with your teeth.

During the cooking, the liquid will reduce, which is fine; but if it reduces to less than half its original quantity, add a little hot water. Because the pieces of meat on the bottom of the Dutch oven will cook somewhat quicker than those higher up, interchange their positions halfway through.

The mushrooms: If you use dried mushrooms, wash them well under running water, put them in a pot with water to cover them, and simmer for thirty minutes or longer. Set them aside. When cool, strain but reserve the liquid. Cut the mushrooms into thin strips and return to the liquid.

If you use fresh mushrooms, and if they are not sandy, wipe them with a cloth, trim and reject the bottom of the stems, and, without peeling, cut them into thin slices. Heat one tablespoon of butter and one tablespoon of oil in a skillet. Add the mushrooms and sauté them uncovered until done—about six minutes—stirring from time to time. Set aside.

When the meat is tender, remove the pieces to a warm plate. Strain the sauce, pressing so that some of the vegetable bits go through to provide a natural thickening agent. Remove and reject 98 percent of the fat from the surface of the sauce. Wash the Dutch oven. Put the meat back into it, add the mushrooms (and liquid, if dried ones were used) and the gravy, and keep hot until time to serve.

To serve: Serve with mashed or boiled potatoes and carrots Burgundy style (p. 196), braised lettuce, or grilled tomatoes (p. 187).

Note: Some people thicken the sauce of this dish with flour. It doesn't hurt the dish, but it does detract from the unctuousness of the natural gravy.

I am aware that the direction to cook for from slightly over two hours to slightly over three hours is not very helpful, but I am basing the time on experience. An easy way to handle the variation in cooking time—and, incidentally, serve dinner on time—is to make the dish the day before. It actually improves, and one can get all the excess fat from the surface of the gravy. Keep the pot in the refrigerator and be sure it is well covered.

MEAT LOAF

The following recipe is for a tried-and-true meat loaf, hot or cold. Although it is not expensive to make, it is not an economy dish either; good-quality ground round steak generally comes high. However, except for a slight loss in weight during the cooking, there is no waste. (I consider this loss a culinary gain since it results from the fat in the meat draining into the sauce, to be later skimmed away.)

INGREDIENTS FOR SIX

2 lb good-quality round steak, twice ground

1 bunch scallions (with half the green part), finely chopped

3 Tbsp carrot, grated

2 Tbsp celery, grated

½ lb mushrooms, finely chopped

2 Tbsp parsley, very finely chopped

2 egg yolks

½ cup dry white bread crumbs

⅛ tsp dried leaf thyme

⅛ tsp dried leaf basil

3 Tbsp butter, oil, or margarine

2 bay leaves

salt and pepper

FOR THE SAUCE

2½ cups beef or chicken bouillon

2 Tbsp tomato paste

½ cup white wine or a dash or two of dry Madeira wine (Wine added to the sauce helps the flavor, but is not essential.)

To make: Preheat the oven to 325°. In a skillet lightly brown the scallions, carrot, and celery in the butter. Turn down heat to very low and cook, covered, until the mixture is practically a puree. This is the most important phase of the cooking, so don't hurry it. Add the mushrooms, thyme, basil, salt, and pepper and cook, covered, for ten minutes more. Add the ground steak, parsley, egg yolks, and bread crumbs to the cooked mixture and put into a large bowl. Mix thoroughly, at first with a large spoon, then with your hands. Form the mixture into a loaf in a glass fireproof dish, leaving room at the sides for the sauce. Press the bay leaves into the top of the loaf. Mix the tomato paste into the bouillon and pour it over the meat loaf. Bake, uncovered, for one hour and ten minutes in a 325° oven. As sauce evaporates, add more bouillon, one-half cup at a time.

To serve: Allow the meat loaf to rest for fifteen minutes out of the oven. Before serving, remove the fat from the sauce and reject it. Meat loaf may be cooked in advance and kept in the refrigerator; again, this facilitates removing the fat which will congeal on top of the sauce. Either reheat or serve cold. Served hot, mashed potatoes are an almost obligatory accompaniment; served cold, it goes well with green salad, sliced tomatoes, and potato chips.

ZRAZY

There are many versions of Polish *zrazy*, but this is the one I like best. If you didn't have to do the meat slicing yourself, I could say that it is an easy dish to prepare, but, frankly, I don't believe there is a butcher in the neighborhood who would slice the meat for you as it should be. If you know such a butcher, don't tell a soul and wish him good health the next time you see him.

INGREDIENTS FOR EIGHT TO TEN

4½ lb round steak (Remove and reject all the fat and gristle. Cut the meat against the grain into very thin slices, three by four inches in size. If the meat is thin enough, the slices may be somewhat smaller; they should not be larger. Put the slices between two pieces of waxed paper and pound them, but not too forcefully, with the bottom of a heavy pot.)

2 bunches scallions (with half the green parts), very finely chopped

1 cup dried bread crumbs, not toasted

½ lb butter

beef bouillon (enough to cover the rolls when combined with the wine)

¼ cup dry Madeira wine

juice of ½ lemon

piece of bay leaf, the size of a dime

salt and pepper

4 Tbsp parsley or 2 Tbsp each parsley and dill, very finely chopped

½ pint sour cream

To make: Sauté the scallions over low heat in half a stick (one-eighth pound) of butter until they are quite soft, but not browned. Add the bread crumbs, mix thoroughly, and continue to sauté gently for a few minutes. If the crumbs remain dry, add a little more butter. Add salt and pepper and set the mixture aside to cool. Then put a bit (about one-half teaspoon) of the mixture on each slice and roll as firmly as possible. Fix each slice with a toothpick. (Technically, the slices should be tied with thread to permit browning on all sides, but it is a chore to tie them and a worse chore to remove the threads later. However, if you are up to it, by all means do so. If held together with toothpicks, however, the rolls can only be browned on two sides.)

Preheat the oven to 300°. In a clean skillet, heat the remaining butter and brown the meat rolls, five or six at a time. Remove to a dish and brown the next batch, until they are all browned. Place them in an ovenproof dish in one or more layers and add the stock, wine, piece of bay leaf, and lemon juice. The liquid should cover the rolls. Cover the dish with aluminum foil and cook in a 300° oven until tender—about one hour, or a little more. In any case, test with a fork after an hour. Before serving, remove excess fat from the surface of the gravy. Sprinkle with the chopped parsley or the mixture of parsley and dill. If you use thread, remove before serving. Otherwise, let the guests remove the toothpicks.

To serve: Serve with *kasha* (p. 195) and baked or mashed potatoes. For a buffet, keep the *zrazy* and garnish hot and offer sour cream, which goes well with the *kasha*, potatoes, and meat. *Zrazy* may be made well in advance and leftovers freeze well.

BEEF GOULASH

What is an authentic goulash to one Hungarian is not necessarily authentic to another. The only thing about this goulash that is at all authentic is that I insist on taking the responsibility for it.

INGREDIENTS FOR FOUR

2 lb lean chuck beef or round steak, cut in pieces the size of a walnut

2 medium onions, chopped

4 to 6 Italian peppers (Buy the sort that are long, pointed, and light green. Remove and reject the stems, seeds, and membranes. Cut the peppers into pieces the size of a fifty-cent piece.)

4 medium potatoes, peeled and roughly chopped

3 medium tomatoes or 1½ cups canned plum tomatoes (If you use fresh tomatoes, peel and seed them and chop roughly. If you use canned tomatoes, put them through a sieve.)

3 Tbsp butter or oil

1 Tbsp paprika or more, to taste

1 tsp caraway seeds

1 medium bay leaf

salt and pepper

water or beef stock to just cover the meat

sour cream

To make: Put the butter or oil in a heavy-bottomed, four-quart pot and heat it. Add the onions and cook them over low heat until they are soft, but not browned. Add the meat and all the other ingredients except the potatoes and the sour cream. Cover the pot and cook over low heat for one hour and fifteen minutes. If at that time the meat seems almost tender, add the potatoes and continue cooking until they are done—a matter of some twenty minutes. If the meat is not tender, cook it a little longer and then add the potatoes.

To serve: Have the sour cream available on the table; some people like a little of it, others like a great deal. If, say, for a buffet dinner, you wish to present this dish a little more elegantly, lift out the pieces of meat and strain the gravy (or sauce, if you will). Return the meat to the gravy, serve with homemade noodles (p. 11), and pass sour cream.

SPAGHETTI SAUCE

One summer afternoon when my wife and I and friends were planning to have charcoal-grilled steak after a ride in the country, my wife suddenly changed her mind and demanded pasta with a sauce. Since we had already bought the steaks and there was no other meat at hand (although there were tomato paste and pasta), I cut the fillet section from two of the porterhouse steaks and, using these as a base, concocted this sauce, which, if I may say so, turned out well. I use it often. It is particularly good on spaghettini or vermicelli, which must be cooked *al dente*—not a fraction too little or a fraction too much, which, with very thin pasta, takes practice. However, the sauce goes well with any pasta, even the very thick sort. Serve with grated cheese if you wish, but in my opinion the cheese detracts from the delicacy of the sauce.

INGREDIENTS FOR FOUR

1 lb fillet of beef or shell (New York) steak (This weight is after all fat, gristle, and bone have been removed. Chop the meat fine with a knife, but do not grind it; when cooked in the sauce, it should not have the grainy texture of ground meat.)

4 very thin slices of best-quality cooked ham, cut in very thin strips

1½ Tbsp each butter and olive oil

8 shallots or one bunch scallions, very finely chopped (If you use scallions, reject the green parts.)

1 7-ounce can tomato paste, less one Tbsp (The sauce is not heavy with tomato.)

piece of bay leaf, the size of a dime

pinch of leaf thyme (about ⅟₁₆ tsp)

1 clove

light sprinkling of celery salt (about ⅟₁₆ tsp)

⅕ tsp mace or nutmeg, ground

enough good-quality beef or chicken stock to make a rather thin sauce (If you wish, do as I do; use half stock and half white wine.)

salt (Use very little; the ham is salty.)

1½ Tbsp flour, blended with cold water until smooth

To make: Heat the butter and oil in a heavy saucepan, add the beef, and cook over medium heat until the meat turns color, stirring frequently. Add the shallots or scallions and cook until they are somewhat soft, but not browned. Add all the rest of the ingredients except the ham and the flour and water mixture. Simmer over low heat for thirty minutes. Add the flour and water mixture after fifteen minutes, pouring it in very slowly and stirring constantly until thoroughly blended. Add the ham two minutes before serving.

Note: The flour mixture produces a sauce that coats the pasta, which I prefer to a sauce that permits the pasta to stand apart—all shiny and oily.

VEAL

MANY AMERICANS who eat veal regularly are not aware that what they buy is not real veal, which is so dissimilar that it appears to have come from a different animal. It is light in color—lighter than chicken breasts—and very tender and tasty. The common run of veal in the United States is a sort of immature beef, which when cooked thoroughly, as veal should be, becomes overdone and dry; when cooked to the rare stage, as beef should be, it is as tough as someone's arm. There is a simple explanation for the difference in meat from the same animal. The best-quality veal is from calves that have been fed only milk and eggs: a trace of red in the meat indicates that the animal has eaten solid food. Why the people who raise calves insist on the inferior type, which brings much lower prices, I don't know. In any case, one is helpless except to buy veal from a butcher who sells the real thing—unfortunately at high prices.

A PROVENÇAL STUFFING

This Provençal dressing is for stuffing boned breast of veal or boned shoulder of lamb, but it is equally good cooked separately and served with a roasted or grilled leg of lamb.

INGREDIENTS FOR SIX

2 slices cooked ham (2 ounces), finely chopped

1 cup celery (with a few leaves), finely chopped

1 bunch scallions (with one-third of the green part), roughly chopped

1 cup unpeeled zucchini (with the soft center part removed and rejected), finely chopped

½ cup mushrooms, sliced

1½ cups fresh spinach (without stems), chopped

3 Tbsp olive oil

½ cup white bread crumbs, dried

½ cup beef or chicken bouillon

1 large clove garlic, chopped

1 egg yolk

2 Tbsp parsley, very finely chopped

2 Tbsp fresh basil leaves or ½ tsp dried basil

salt and pepper

[143]

To make: Heat the olive oil, and add the celery, scallions, garlic, and ham. Cook, covered, for ten minutes over very low heat, shaking the pan from time to time. Then add the zucchini and mushrooms, placing them on top of the first mixture. Place spinach on top of the first two mixtures. Cover and cook for fifteen minutes. Remove cover, add parsley and basil, and mix the entire contents of the pan thoroughly. Allow to cool until tepid. Mix the bread crumbs with the bouillon and squeeze dry. Put the egg yolk, crumbs, salt, pepper, and the pan mixture into a bowl and mix well. Do not pack the stuffing too tightly, as it will swell during cooking. To cook separately, place in a covered pan and bake in a 300° oven for one hour.

AILLADE DE VEAU

An old Provençal classic, *aillade de veau* is quite garlicky, but the garlic in this dish is cooked for at least one hour and fifteen minutes, so that the flavor is there but not the redolent odor. However, if the very idea of a lot of garlic puts you off, use shallots or scallions instead. Of the two alternates, shallots are best: they have the good qualities of both garlic and onions without the strong odor of either. Whichever variety of the bulb you choose to use, try this dish. At best, veal is bland and this preparation does something special for it. In fact, I'm quite sure you will find it delicious. (Note the characteristically French restraint in the quantity of tomato used, even though this recipe is from Provence, where they grow the best tomatoes in the world.)

INGREDIENTS FOR FOUR

2 to 2½ lb lean, boneless veal, cut up as for stew

2 Tbsp olive oil

1½ Tbsp dried, untoasted bread crumbs

*12 cloves garlic, peeled, or the same number of
shallots or scallions (If you use scallions, retain
just a bit of the green parts.)*

*2 medium-sized ripe tomatoes, peeled, seeded, and
chopped*

piece of laurel (bay) leaf, the size of a dime

⅛ tsp leaf thyme, dried

¼ tsp leaf tarragon, dried

dry white wine, enough to cover the meat

salt and pepper

To make: Drop the tomatoes in a pot of boiling water
for no more than thirty seconds. Then put them in a
colander and pour cold water over them. With a sharp
knife, remove and reject the hard stem parts. Peel the
tomatoes, cut them in half, and squeeze them to get rid
of the seeds. Inspect the tomatoe halves; if any seeds
still remain, remove them with a blunt knife or the
handle of a spoon. Then chop the tomatoes.

Pour one-half tablespoon of olive oil in a pot and
heat over low flame. Add the garlic, shallots, or scallions and cook them for five minutes, stirring from
time to time. Add the chopped tomatoes, laurel, thyme,
tarragon, salt, and pepper. Cook for fifteen minutes.

In another, and larger, pot brown the veal in the
remaining one and one-half tablespoons of olive oil.

When the veal has been well browned on all sides, add the bread crumbs and, stirring rapidly, cook for two more minutes.

Now combine the tomato mixture with the meat, add the white wine to cover, and cook over very low heat until tender. This should not take more than one hour and fifteen minutes, but test with a fork to be sure.

To serve: Aillade de veau goes well with rice. If you have a large platter or serving dish, make a border around the edge of the dish with the rice. Pour or spoon the *aillade* into the center of the dish, and there you are. It wouldn't hurt to sprinkle the finished dish with very, very finely chopped parsley.

SAUTÉED VEAL SCHNITZEL

Sautéed veal schnitzel is certainly the most popular of all veal preparations and the easiest to make—that is, if you have good veal, sliced very thin from the leg, and if the meat is not overmoist. In my general discussion of veal (see p. 142) I stress the desirability of using the variety that is very white, but I am only too well aware that that sort of veal is not generally available. Another reason why this is such a useful recipe is that even less than first-quality veal comes out rather well.

INGREDIENTS FOR FOUR

*4 veal schnitzels (slices), cut from a leg of veal
(They should be cut on the bias, very thin, and,
ideally, large enough to practically hang over the
edge of a large dinner plate.)*

small bowl of flour

2 eggs, lightly beaten

small bowl of untoasted bread crumbs

2 Tbsp butter, or more

salt and pepper

lemons, quartered (for garnishing)

To make: Pare the meat of any membranes and fat
that can be removed without deforming the slices, and
place them between doubled and folded waxed paper.
Pound them with whatever seems suitable to you,
although I suggest a large, heavy pot with a large
bottom and certain heft. However, don't get carried
away with this process; the idea is to flatten the meat,
not pulverize it. Dip each schnitzel in the flour, making
sure that every bit of the surface of the meat is covered
and also that all excess flour is shaken off. After dipping in the flour, dip the schnitzel into the beaten eggs
and then into the bread crumbs. The last step is the
crucial one. Nothing looks less appetizing than an improperly breaded whatever—moth-eaten is what comes
to mind. Very carefully press the crumbs uniformly over
the entire surface of the schnitzel, pressing the crumbs
in when necessary. As each schnitzel is breaded, put it
on a grill in the refrigerator. Cook the schnitzels just
before serving them.

In a large, low-sided skillet—or two skillets, depending

on how many schnitzels you are cooking and their size
—melt at least two tablespoons of butter. When the
butter is hot and just beginning to turn light brown,
add the schnitzels. Cook over moderate heat and turn
with a spatula; they should be golden brown, but not
frazzled. The result should very crisp, but juicy, schnitzels and, if the directions have been followed correctly,
they will not be at all greasy.

To serve: Season with salt and pepper. Serve with
quartered lemons and no other garnish. Some cooks
place a slice of lemon in the center of the schnitzels,
with a rolled anchovy stuffed with a caper on the slice
of lemon. The French name schnitzels with this garnish
escalopes de veau à la Liégeoise. German restaurants
add a poached egg, which strikes me as redundant.

VEAL CHOPS PAPRIKA

INGREDIENTS FOR FOUR

4 thick, first-quality veal chops

*¼ lb Hungarian bacon (fatback), very thinly
sliced, lightly smoked, with paprika pressed into
the fat (Anything comparable will do in its place.)*

1 medium onion, finely chopped

*1½ tsp paprika (Real paprika, and not red dust,
is required.)*

1½ cups chicken stock, heated

1 cup sour cream

½ tsp salt

To make: Lightly brown the bacon, push it aside, and
brown the chops well. Turn down the heat and brown

the onion gently. Add the heated stock, paprika, and salt and cook, covered, over a low fire for about twenty minutes or until done. Just before serving, add the sour cream.

To serve: A few croutons fried in butter and a little chopped parsley provide a reasonable garnish for this dish.

SAUTÉED VEAL WITH MARSALA

Veal sautéed in Marsala wine is distinctly Italian. Servings for four can be made in ten minutes. However, as with all seemingly transparent recipes, everything depends on the quality of the ingredients and a light hand.

INGREDIENTS FOR FOUR

1 lb 6 ounces very thin scallops of veal (These should be cut from the leg, slightly on the bias. It is best to buy this sort of veal from a German or Italian butcher, and, if you can find one who handles the very fine, white variety, so much the better.)

½ cup dry Marsala wine (There are concoctions labeled cream of Marsala and other fantasies on the market. Avoid them; they fall in the category of what W. E. Massee, the well known wine and food expert, calls "the soda fountain approach to wine.")

4 Tbsp butter

juice of ½ lemon

salt and pepper

flour

½ cup chicken stock

To make: Cut the veal into pieces the size of a silver dollar and flatten each piece. To do this, cover the meat with waxed paper and pound it lightly with the bottom of a heavy pot. If the meat is too moist, spread the pieces on paper towels until needed. Ten minutes before you want to serve the dish, dip each miniature scallop into flour, making sure each piece is well, but lightly, coated. Heat the butter in a large frying pan and, when the butter is hot, begin cooking the meat. Cook until each piece is nicely browned on both sides. Cook as many pieces as you can without crowding the pan and, of course, they should not touch each other. Turn with a spatula. As the pieces are cooked, remove them to a hot platter and add salt and pepper. If you need more butter during the cooking, add it in small pats. When all the meat has been removed to the platter, add the Marsala wine, chicken stock, and lemon juice to the pan. Over highest heat, working swiftly, scrape the bottom of the pan with the spatula until all the browned bits are blended into the sauce.

To serve: Pour the sauce over the meat. Serve with chopped spinach, flavored with salt, pepper, butter, and a few drops of lemon juice.

LAMB

IN THE UNITED STATES, for reasons I have not been able to determine, sheep enjoy a sort of Peter Pan status—lambs never attain muttonhood. The late Mr. Lucius Beebe, a mutton enthusiast if there ever was one and a most entertaining writer for *Gourmet* magazine, has recounted his experience in tracing to their source mutton chops he enjoyed in a well-known San Francisco restaurant. When he did manage to contact the restaurant's supplier and asked the obvious questions, he met with the following response: "Mutton! We don't handle mutton; those were just big old lamb chops." Certainly, it doesn't make any difference what meat is called as long as it is enjoyed, but aware people surely notice the vast difference in size between baby or spring lamb and the hefty legs of "lamb" one sees in the supermarkets. I must point out, however, that genuinely young lamb, like genuine veal, must be cooked very well to be edible, while a seven-pound leg of "lamb," for example, is at its best when served rare.

For those who find that lamb tastes too much like lamb—and I have tasted lamb that had almost the flavor of a sheepskin glove—may I suggest a marinade Alice Toklas developed to perfection: Port wine (good quality, imported) in the quantity of two cups for a six-pound leg, one bunch of scallions, chopped, a few leaves of thyme and rosemary, a small bay leaf, and the juice of one-half a small lemon. Marinate the lamb in this mixture for twenty-four hours, turning the meat from time to time. Use the marinade for basting during the cooking.

ROAST LEG OF LAMB WITH GARLIC PUREE

If the idea of a puree of garlic makes you nervous, be assured that this particular puree is mild. Since the puree is served separately along with the sauce made from the meat and vegetable juices, everyone has a choice.

INGREDIENTS FOR SIX

6½ lb leg of lamb

1 tsp leaf thyme

2 medium bay leaves

1 stalk celery (with half its leaves)

1 lemon, cut in half

3 Tbsp butter

2 medium carrots, finely chopped

1 shallot or 2 scallions, finely chopped

1 clove garlic, finely chopped

salt and pepper

⅛ tsp nutmeg, grated

few drops of lemon juice

12 triangles (half slices) of white bread (with the crusts removed), sautéed in butter until brown and crisp

butter to sauté bread triangles

FOR THE SAUCE

10 ounces garlic cloves, peeled but left whole

2 Tbsp heavy cream

salt and pepper

To make: Preheat the oven to 500°. Rub the leg of lamb well on all sides with the lemon halves. Put it in a roasting pan and cook for twenty minutes in a 500° oven, which will melt some of the fat. Pour the fat off and reject it. Then make two vertical cuts in the meat, right next to the bone on the shank end, and insert the bay leaves. Add the butter, celery, carrots, shallot, garlic, and nutmeg to the pan. Sprinkle the meat with the leaf thyme and put the roast back in a 350° oven. Cook for one hour and twenty-five minutes more, or until the meat is done to suit you. Baste frequently. If you use a meat thermometer, the meat will be cooked medium at between 145° to 150°. If you like lamb well done, cook it until the thermometer registers 160°. Before serving the roast, allow it to rest for at least ten minutes (see p. 274).

While the lamb is roasting, blanch the garlic cloves in boiling water for five minutes. Drain them, rinse in cold water, put back in the pot, cover with cold water, and boil for five more minutes. Drain them again. Add the cream, salt, and pepper, and puree in a blender; or put the garlic through a vegetable mill, and then add the salt, pepper, and cream. Mix well and serve in a separate sauce dish.

After you have removed the roast to a platter and while it is resting, strain the pan juices from the roasting pan, remove the fat, add a few drops of lemon juice, and serve in a sauce-boat.

To serve: Sauté the bread triangles, arrange them around the sliced leg of lamb, and serve.

GRILLED LAMB KIDNEYS

Grilled lamb kidneys are a well-established restaurant standby in Paris and for good reason—almost everyone likes them. They take but a few minutes to cook, and their characteristic *vert pré* garnish of shoestring potatoes and watercress is always at hand, since the same garnish is used for other restaurant standbys, such as *entrecôte* (rib steak) and other grilled meats. There is nothing banal about lamb kidneys; they are very expensive in France (which leads me to believe that they can't be much prized in America because I can buy them here for a fraction of the cost in France). This seems to indicate that there are a good many people in the United States who have never tasted the delicate, nutlike flavor of a perfectly grilled lamb kidney, beautifully browned on the outside, slightly pink inside, and very juicy. Try it once; not much expense is involved, and it might be a revelation to you.

INGREDIENTS FOR SIX

12 lamb kidneys (with the parchmentlike membrane removed and rejected), split horizontally from the thickest end, but not cut through

3 Tbsp olive oil

1 bunch watercress

2 cans shoestring potatoes, or more

juice of ½ small lemon

salt and pepper

¼ lb butter

1 Tbsp parsley, very, very finely chopped

To make: Open the two halves of each kidney and keep open by threading them on metal or wooden spits. Brush them with olive oil and place cut-side down on a grill resting on a pan or a doubled piece of heavy aluminum foil. Put the kidneys under a broiler about four inches from the heat and cook until they are brown and firm.

Turn them over and cook until just firm. This should not take more than five minutes per side, but broiler heats vary. Check one of the kidneys by cutting into it with a sharp knife; the outside should be firm, the inside slightly pink but definitely cooked. While the kidneys are cooking, prepare a *beurre à la maître d'hôtel* by mixing the butter, parsley, lemon, salt, and pepper. Mash these ingredients together until they form a homogenous blend. Chill the mixture in the refrigerator.

Remove and reject the heavy stems of the watercress and flavor the leaves simply with lemon juice, salt, and pepper.

A few minutes before the kidneys are done, heat the shoestring potatoes in their cans, but, again, don't forget to open one end.

To serve: Arrange the kidneys on one end of a heated oval platter. Divide the *beurre à la maître d'hôtel* into twenty-four parts, putting an equal amount into each half-kidney. Arrange the shoestring potatoes and then the watercress on the platter. Pour the juice from the kidneys over the kidneys.

SHISH KEBAB

There are several ways of preparing the popular shish kebab. The least practical is to cook a variety of vegetables—onions, mushrooms, peppers, tomatoes, and sometimes eggplant—on the same skewers as the meat. All of these vegetables take different lengths of time to cook, and cooking them simultaneously naturally produces a variety of textures, which can range from mushy, even disintegrating tomatoes to scorched, but underdone onions. There is also the matter of marinating the meat, which is often too heavyhanded with a coarse, overspiced marinade. If the meat is good— and if it isn't, there is very little point in making shish kebab—one should be able to taste it. If it isn't good, marinating it will not transform it into anything other than it is.

Shish kebab is best cooked over a charcoal fire, but I have frequently cooked it in an oven broiler with what my guests have pronounced notable success. Here is my method.

INGREDIENTS FOR SIX

2½ to 3 lb leg of lamb, cut in strips 1½ inches long and ½ inch wide (The meat should be absolutely free of fat, tendons, and nerves.)

30 small white onions of uniform size, peeled

18 small mushrooms of uniform size (Wipe them with a damp cloth, and trim and reject the stem ends.)

2 large green peppers, cut into strips the size of the pieces of meat (Reject the seeds and membranes inside the peppers. I peel the peppers, but this refinement is optional.)

6 small tomatoes, halved (Brush with olive oil and dust with a little leaf thyme, salt, and pepper.)

salt

FOR THE MARINADE

juice of 2 medium lemons

¾ cup olive oil

4 sprigs parsley (both stems and leaves)

2 small bay leaves, broken up

½ tsp leaf thyme, dried

pepper, to taste (I prefer ⅛ tsp of cayenne pepper.)

*If you like garlic, add as much as you wish. I like garlic
very much, but not in this dish.*

FOR THE RICE

2 cups good-quality rice

4 cups bouillon or water

1 Tbsp olive oil

juice of ½ lemon

salt

2 Tbsp butter, cut in small pieces

To make: Put the ingredients for the marinade into a
large bowl and mix well. Add the lamb, onions, mushrooms, and peppers and mix, making sure each piece is
coated. Set aside in a cool place for one hour, mixing
from time to time.

When you are ready to cook the shish kebab, put the
onions on a doubled piece of heavy aluminum foil,
turned up at the sides. Cook under the broiler until just
soft and brown, turning several times. Cover the onions
with the pieces of green pepper and, when the peppers
are half done, put the mushrooms on top. Cook until
the mushrooms are tender, but not frazzled. Meanwhile,
put the meat on six disposable bamboo skewers (sold
in Japanese shops) or on metal skewers. Thread the
meat by piercing first one end of the strip of meat and
then the other, pressing the pieces together. Place the
skewers on another piece of doubled foil. Remove the
cooked vegetables from under the broiler and keep them
warm in the oven. Put the meat under the broiler. Then
dip the halved tomatoes into what is left of the marinade, place cut-side up on another piece of foil, and

put under the broiler beside the meat. Turn the meat so that it browns on all sides, but do not overcook. Do not turn the tomatoes. If the tomatoes are done before the meat, remove them from under the broiler and keep them warm in the oven with the other vegetables.

To cook the rice (which should be started ten minutes before the vegetable-meat procedures), wash it very well in cold water, drain, and put in a pot. Add the bouillon or water, olive oil, lemon juice, and salt and bring to a boil. Stir very well; then turn down the heat as low as it will go. Cover the pot well and cook for twenty minutes. Do not stir. Test a grain by pressing it between your thumb and forefinger; if the center of the grain is soft, the rice is cooked. (All the liquid will have been absorbed by the rice, so don't be alarmed if the rice is a bit crisp on the bottom. Don't serve the crisp bottom part, although in the Far East it is considered a delicacy.) Just before putting the rice on a platter, mix in the butter while fluffing up the rice.

To serve: Pile the rice in a dome on a platter. Put the meat skewers on top, arranging them in a row, and pour the meat juices over them. (The guests remove the meat from the skewers.) Arrange the vegetables around the meat with the tomatoes in a ring around the outside of the platter. Pour all the vegetable juices over the vegetables. Only now, salt the meat and vegetables. Serve very hot. Have lemons, quartered and seeded, on the table for those who like more lemon.

Note: Once you try this recipe, you will find that (after mastering the routine) there is very little to it. Because the meat and vegetable juices are not carbonized in the flames of a grill, the dish has an exquisite flavor. And each ingredient will be of just the right texture.

PORK

IN FRANCE, and in Europe generally, pork does not stand very high in the ranking of meats for entrees, despite the fact that pork *per se* figures in almost every meal in some way—in the form of larding for a fillet of beef or a roast of veal, as an essential ingredient in a pâté or a sausage, as a lubricant (in the shape of barding) for the breasts of game birds, or in innumerable other combinations in which no other fat will do. Pork fat keeps other meats juicy without imparting its own flavor. It pleases me, however, that we don't have the European prejudice about pork and can thus enjoy a crown roast of pork—to me, one of the great delicacies—without having qualms about its socio-culinary status.

BREADED PORK CHOPS

Breaded pork chops are not an item of *la haute cuisine*, but I like them and they make a nice winter, family luncheon entree. The problem is to find good-quality pork chops, which, surprisingly enough, can be done in supermarkets. It is a matter of choosing the right ones—a task easier said than done. As a basic guide, the meat should be almost white and not coarsely textured, and it should come from a small animal. When you get the chops home, unwrap them, wipe with a damp cloth, and loosely wrapped in waxed paper, refrigerate for at least twelve hours.

INGREDIENTS FOR FOUR

4 very thick pork chops (Bone them, remove and reject the fat, and split the chops in two against the grain. Put the slices between sheets of waxed paper and flatten them well with the bottom of a heavy pot.)

2 eggs, lightly beaten

flour

bread crumbs, dried but not toasted

salt and pepper

oil, as needed

butter, as needed

To make: Heat the oil and butter in a large skillet—or in two skillets. Use only enough oil and butter to properly lubricate the crumbs coating the chops; it is better to begin with a little and add more as required. Dip each slice into the flour, making sure all the surfaces are covered. Shake off any excess flour. Dip each chop into the beaten eggs and then into the crumbs, pressing the crumbs into the meat; there should be no bare spots. Sauté the breaded slices over low heat until nicely browned on both sides, turning as often as necessary. To test whether they are cooked through, make a small cut with a sharp knife in one of the chops. If necessary, they may be kept warm in the oven.

To serve: Season with salt and pepper. Serve with applesauce, mashed potatoes, and *cauliflower à la polonaise*.

ROAST LOIN OF PORK SERVED COLD
WITH PRUNES AND APPLESAUCE

Cold roast pork is much more popular in France than in the United States, probably because it simply has not entered our day-to-day repertoire. Prepared as indicated in this recipe, it is a nice addition to a buffet lunch and is surprisingly delicate.

INGREDIENTS FOR FIVE OR SIX FOR LUNCHEON
OR AS PART OF A BUFFET

1 5-lb loin of pork, boned and tied. Have the butcher remove excess fat from the meat.

3 large scallions (white part only)

salt and pepper

⅛ tsp thyme

10 very large prunes, pits removed

3 golden delicious apples

To make: Preheat the oven to 325°. With a sharp knife, make deep incisions all over the meat. Cut the scallions into not-too-small slivers and insert them into the incisions. Salt and pepper the meat and dust it with thyme. Put the roast in a roasting pan on a grill and put it in the oven for a little less than three hours (approximately thirty-five minutes per pound). If you use a meat thermometer, the meat will be done when the thermometer reads 175°. Allow the roast to cool in a cool place, but not in the refrigerator.

Cook the prunes according to the instructions on the package, but do not add sugar. They should not be overcooked. Chill them in the refrigerator.

Peel and core the apples. Slice the apples and cook them until just soft in a little water to which you have added two and one-half tablespoons of sugar. Mash them thoroughly with a potato masher and chill.

To serve: As neatly as possible slice the pork into medium-thin slices (before or after removing the string, depending on how well you carve). Place the slices in overlapping fashion on one-half of an oval platter. In the center of the other half of the platter, make a dome of the applesauce. Drain the prunes well, press them flat to form medallions, and dispose them in a half-circle around the applesauce.

ROAST PORK WITH GARLIC AND CARAWAY SEEDS

Most people like roast pork; and, while I should perhaps be ashamed to say it, I am so bored with prime
ribs of beef I welcome a crisp, succulent, not-too-fat,
well-flavored slice of roast pork with a garnish as simple as mashed potatoes and applesauce. Pork goes well
with many things: sauerkraut, applesauce, roast potatoes, creamy onions, sweet potatoes, cauliflower *à la
polonaise*, glazed carrots, and onions browned with the
roast. This recipe is particularly tasty served with sauerkraut and boiled potatoes.

INGREDIENTS FOR FIVE

*1 5-lb loin of pork. Have the butcher cut through
the chine bone.*

1 Tbsp caraway seeds

2 cloves garlic, cut into slivers

salt and pepper

To make: Preheat the oven to 325°. Make incisions in
the meat, and insert the garlic slivers into them. Dust
the entire roast with salt, pepper, and thyme. Put the
roast on a grill in a roasting pan and bake for a little
less than three hours. If you use a meat thermometer,
the meat will be done when the thermometer reads
175°. Allow the roast to rest for at least fifteen minutes
before carving (see p. 275 for an improvised warming
oven).

To serve: Carve the roast into fairly thick slices and
serve with any of the above-mentioned garnishes.

COMPOSED DISHES

THE TERM *composed dishes* in the context of this book means nothing more than combinations that go well together, such as the dish on page 179: cabbage with Canadian bacon and boiled potatoes. Cabbage, although often thought to be strong in odor (only if cooked over too high heat) and seemingly strong in flavor, is really bland, which is why cabbage is also served with corned beef. There are many such combinations in every country's cuisine, some of which excite me not at all: for example, the Scandinavian fondness for herring and

boiled potatoes, or the French, Spanish, and Portu-
guese preoccupation with salted codfish, a delicacy
which to my palate has all the allure of a fishy-flavored
braised newspaper. Another singular combination I
never saw before I came to New York is poached eggs
with mashed potatoes. This, it turns out, has a genuine
raison d'être; it is one of the standbys of people suffer-
ing from ulcers.

ROAST BEEF HASH

This roast beef hash, unlike most, is not greasy and
is ideal for breakfast, brunch, or lunch.

INGREDIENTS FOR EIGHT

*4 cups cooked roast beef, chopped medium fine
(Rare beef is best. Trim off and reject all fat,
gristle, and dried or overdone parts.)*

6 cups boiled potatoes, chopped medium fine

*1 bunch scallions (with half the green parts), finely
chopped*

½ cup heavy cream

½ cup beef bouillon

salt and pepper

4 Tbsp butter

To make: Sauté the scallions in one tablespoon butter.
Cook, covered, over very low heat until they are soft,
but not brown. Mix together the scallions, beef, potatoes, bouillon, cream, salt, and pepper. Melt one tablespoon butter in a shallow ovenproof dish. Add the hash
mixture, pressing down so that it forms a firm cake.

Chop the remaining butter and distribute it on top of the hash. Cook under a broiler until brown and crisp. If you like more brown crust, fold in the first crust, sprinkle the top with a little more chopped butter, and cook until brown. If, for any reason, you can't serve the hash immediately, keep it in an oven set at very low temperature. This dish may also be baked in a 350° oven for twenty-five minutes.

Some people like green pepper in hash. If you decide to use it, chop the pepper very fine and cook with the scallions. If the idea of peeling the pepper isn't too radical for you, do so with a sharp knife; it helps avoid the unpleasant characteristic that green peppers and certain other foods have of "repeating."

Note: For corned beef hash, follow precisely the same procedure with corned beef substituted for roast beef. If you prefer to cook the hash in patties, make them small; large patties tend to look gross.

SCOTCH COLLOPS MEAT PIE

In the accepted sense of what a meat pie is (a fricassee or a stew in a crust), Scotch collops is not a meat pie at all. But it is as meaty as a meat pie can be, since it consists of nothing more than ground beef and scallions in a crust. If the ground beef and onions remind you of the familiar hamburger, you are on the right track. The American hamburger is directly related to a German dish called *Hamburger klops*, a specialty of the North German port of Hamburg, and the connection between *klops* and *collops* is evident. (This pie is called a *tourtière* in French Canada.) Don't let this genealogy put you off; the pie is its own reward. It can be reheated, and it freezes well. Heated and cut in small wedges, it is an ideal cocktail snack.

INGREDIENTS FOR A TEN-INCH PIE

2 lb absolutely lean round steak, ground

3 bunches scallions (with half the green tops), finely chopped

2 Tbsp butter

salt and pepper

puff paste (see p. 227) or pie crust dough for a covered pie

1 egg yolk mixed with 2 Tbsp cream, milk, or water

To make: The key to this dish is to simmer the scallions, salt and pepper, and meat in butter without browning; the scallions should be soft, and the meat should be broken up well with a fork and cooked only until it turns color. Make enough puff paste for a covered pie or use your favorite pie crust dough. Preheat the oven to 400°. Line a ten-inch pie plate with part of the dough, rolled out very thin. Add the meat and scallions and cover with the rest of the dough, rolled out a little thicker than the bottom crust. Brush the dough with an egg yolk mixed with cream, milk, or water. Slash the crust in about four places and cook the pie in a 400° oven until nicely browned.

STUFFED ESCAROLE

Stuffed escarole is a close relative of stuffed cabbage and stuffed vine leaves, just as tasty and slightly more delicate. It can be served as one of the hot dishes of

[168]

a buffet or as an entrée for lunch after a light *hors d'oeuvre varié* or a soup.

INGREDIENTS FOR FOUR

10 ounces lean veal, ground

8 ounces lean pork, ground

4 Tbsp uncooked rice, washed well

1 egg

1 tsp parsley, very finely chopped

pinch of leaf thyme ($\frac{1}{16}$ tsp)

$\frac{1}{16}$ tsp nutmeg, very finely grated

1 large head of escarole

salt and pepper

2 to 3 cups good beef or chicken stock

2 Tbsp tomato paste

juice of $\frac{1}{2}$ lemon

oil

To make: Remove the hard core of the escarole and reject any discolored outside leaves. Drop the escarole in a large pot of boiling water and cook only until the leaves are flexible—a matter of about two minutes. Remove and drain in a colander. While the escarole is draining and cooling, mix well the veal, pork, rice, egg, salt, pepper, parsley, and thyme. Next, appraise the size and number of escarole leaves you have to determine how much filling to use for each roll. If the lower-center parts of the escarole leaves are too stiff to roll properly, cut them out and reject them. With your hands, take some of the meat and rice mixture and roll it into a ball about the size of a very large olive. Put it on one leaf, or on more than one, and carefully roll up, folding in the sides before making the last fold. Put the roll in an ovenproof dish with the fold underneath. Repeat until all the meat is used up. Add a few drops of oil to the pan as you place the rolls side by side. Do not worry about making the rolls tight. As the rice swells during the cooking, they will become smoothly firm. Put the pan on a burner of your stove and, over high heat, brown the bottom of the rolls, but lightly. Do not turn the rolls. Add the stock, tomato paste, nutmeg, and lemon juice and cook over very low heat for one hour and thirty minutes or cook in a 300° oven for the same length of time. Look at the rolls after forty-five minutes. If the stock has reduced to one-half the height of the rolls, add another cup.

Note: If you are fed up with tomato sauces—even one as light as this—omit the tomato paste and add more stock or, better yet, white wine, or a mixture of white wine and dry Madeira. If fresh basil is available, forget the parsley and the thyme. Instead, use at least two tablespoons of basil, which is perfect in dishes such as this. If you like the flavor of tarragon, omit the parsley and thyme and use one-half teaspoon of dried tarragon or one tablespoon of fresh tarragon.

YELLOW SUMMER SQUASH STUFFED WITH CHICKEN

Yellow summer squash is a delicate vegetable, although a trifle watery (some people would call it bland), but when properly cooked and seasoned, it is unbeatable. Unlike some of the more aggressively flavored vegetables, it combines well with other ingredients without overpowering them. The following recipe, I think, demonstrates its possibilities for a sophisticated dish.

INGREDIENTS FOR SIX TO NINE

2 medium chicken breasts, poached (see page 102)

4 cups chicken bouillon

9 yellow squash, uniform in size, scrubbed but not peeled (They should be no larger than a medium cucumber. Cut them in two, lengthwise. Hollow out the halves, leaving a shell just about one-half-inch thick. Reject the pulp.)

2 packages frozen, chopped spinach

1 medium (17-ounce) can Italian pomidori tomatoes, sieved

5 Tbsp flour

5 Tbsp butter

4 Tbsp dry imported Madeira wine

salt and white pepper

To make: Bone and skin the poached chicken breasts. Reject the bones and skin, and cut the meat into neat pieces one and one-half inch by one-half inch. Use a sharp knife; the edges of the meat should not be ragged. Set aside. Thaw the spinach in a pan over lowest heat, using just enough water to moisten the bottom of the pan. Break the blocks of spinach up with a fork, as the heat penetrates them. Do not cook the spinach; when all the lumps have melted, it is done enough for this stage of the recipe. Place the squash halves, cut-side up, in two good-sized shallow baking dishes, preferably glass. Put some of the spinach in each half, portioning it until all is distributed.

[171]

Two sauces are used in this dish. Make the first sauce by cooking two tablespoons flour with two tablespoons butter over low heat, stirring constantly. Do not brown the mixture. When the flour has completely and smoothly absorbed the butter, add the sieved tomatoes, one cup of chicken broth, and salt and pepper to taste. Cook slowly, stirring constantly, until the sauce is thoroughly blended and smooth. Pour this into the squash halves over the spinach, again portioning until it is all used up. Now put the pieces of chicken on top of the spinach and sauce, fitting the pieces in as neatly as possible.

Preheat the oven to 350°. Make the second sauce by cooking the remaining three tablespoons flour and three tablespoons butter, precisely as for the first sauce. Mix in three cups of chicken bouillon, salt and pepper, and cook very slowly until smooth. The sauce should not be too thick. Add the Madeira wine and pour the mixture over the squash, using a ladle to assure proper distribution. Place the dishes in a 350° oven and cook until the squash are tender. Test with a fork after about twenty minutes. Squash do not take long to cook and the idea here is to cook them, not brown the top of the sauce.

Note: If you like the top of the sauce browned, at the last moment sprinkle with a very light dusting of grated Parmesan cheese and brown the dish under the broiler.

SEAFOOD SALAD

Most people like seafood salad, and, when arranged on a large platter, it does make a handsome summer buffet dish. Although boiled lobster is the finest of the main ingredients suggested, poached crab meat, shrimp, and salmon are also excellent. However, in an emergency—and this is an ideal emergency dish—canned lobster, crab, shrimp, or salmon, if of first quality, will make a quite acceptable salad.

INGREDIENTS FOR EIGHT

5 cups or more cooked lobster, crab meat, shrimp, or salmon

16 stalks canned white asparagus, or more

6 medium artichoke hearts, quartered, or 12 very small Italian-type artichokes in oil, or more

10 green olives

10 black olives

6 hard-boiled eggs, peeled and halved

5 medium tomatoes, very ripe, quartered

Boston, Simpson, or Bibb lettuce, or some of all three varieties

1 bunch watercress (without stems)

2 cups homemade mayonnaise (see p. 26)

3 lemons, quartered and seeded

(alternate sour cream dressing)

To make: Tear the lettuce into small pieces, mix it with the watercress, and arrange in a dome on a large platter, leaving two inches bare around the edge of the platter. Arrange your choice of seafood on the top of the dome of greens. Then, working down the sides of the dome, place first a ring of the artichokes, then a ring of black and green olives, then the asparagus, followed by some more olives. Arrange the halved eggs, quartered tomatoes, and quartered lemons around the edge of the platter. Pour or spoon some of the mayonnaise around the seafood, just above the artichokes, and put a dab on each egg half. Serve the remainder separately.

Note: All the ingredients for this salad can be prepared beforehand; in fact, it is best when assembled shortly before serving. If you wonder why white asparagus, and canned at that, is indicated rather than fresh, it is because canned white asparagus have just the right flavor and texture. Use whichever you want.

ALTERNATE SOUR CREAM DRESSING

Sour cream dressing, somewhat lighter than mayonnaise, is a nice change, especially when flavored with dill.

INGREDIENTS

2 cups sour cream

1½ Tbsp fresh dill, very finely chopped, or 1½ tsp dried dill weed

4 Tbsp fresh lemon juice

3 Tbsp olive oil

salt and pepper

To make: Mix all the ingredients together thoroughly.

SPINACH AND RICOTTA CHEESE ON GARLIC TOAST

Spinach and ricotta cheese, a mixture of Italian origin, is usually served in the form of small, egg-shaped dumplings. I suggest my modification of it which, in combination with garlic toast, makes a good, light first course for lunch or dinner. This version does not require flour, since a firm binding agent is not necessary.

INGREDIENTS FOR SIX

2 packages best-quality frozen, chopped spinach

1 lb ricotta cheese

3 egg yolks, lightly beaten

4 Tbsp Parmesan cheese, grated

salt and pepper

FOR THE GARLIC TOAST

18 slices Italian bread, just under ½-inch thick

garlic, put through a press, to taste

¼ lb butter or margarine, softened

5 Tbsp olive oil

salt and pepper

To make: In a heavy-bottomed pan, cook the spinach over low heat, using only enough water to prevent sticking. Turn the blocks of spinach from time to time, and break them up with a fork as they begin to thaw. When the spinach is thoroughly thawed, add salt and pepper and continue cooking for a few minutes. Mix the spinach and the ricotta together, preferably in a

[1 7 5]

blender (although this is not absolutely necessary; a thorough, vigorous mixing with a fork or spoon will do). If you use a blender, you will have to mix in batches. Don't overdo the blending or you will end up with an ethereally aerated mess.

Now reheat the spinach and ricotta mixture. When it is heated through, add the beaten egg yolks and Parmesan cheese and mix well with a fork. Cook over low heat for five minutes, stirring constantly.

To make the garlic toast: Mix the softened butter and olive oil with as much pressed garlic as you like. Add salt and pepper and mix again. Grill one side of the bread slices under the broiler. Spread the garlic-butter-oil mixture on the ungrilled sides of the bread and return to the broiler. Cook until browned as desired. (There will be a moment during the cooking of the garlic side of the bread when the area around the oven will smell pungently of the bulb, but this rapidly changes into a soft, most appetizing odor, which means that the garlic has cooked and is no longer acrid.)

To serve: Arrange three pieces of garlic toast on each of six plates. Distribute the spinach and ricotta mixture as evenly as possible on the toast.

BEEKENOHFE

Beekenohfe, an Alsatian dish, is a casserole of pork shoulder, lamb shoulder, potatoes, onions, bay leaf, thyme, and white Alsatian wine. Its name is spelled in a variety of ways, depending on the locale. This dish is characteristic of the best French regional cooking—the ingredients are ordinary; the flavor is extraordinary. It is ideal for an out-of-doors, early autumn lunch or dinner and is best made in a large, high rather than wide, earthenware pot with a lid. If possible, the vessel should be attractive enough to serve the dish directly from it.

INGREDIENTS FOR EIGHT

2 lb boned shoulder of pork (with most of the fat removed), cut up as for stew

2 lb boned shoulder of lamb (with all the fat removed), cut up as for stew

3 lb firm potatoes, peeled and sliced

1½ lb yellow onions, peeled and chopped

dry, white Alsatian wine, enough to cover the meat and vegetables

1 large bay leaf

¼ tsp leaf thyme

2 Tbsp butter, chopped into small pieces

salt and pepper

To make: Preheat the oven to 350°. To fill the casserole dish, begin with a layer of potatoes, cover them with a layer of the combined pork and lamb, cover the meat with a layer of onions, and add the bay leaf and thyme. Dust each layer with salt and pepper, being careful not to overdo it. Repeat the sequence of potatoes, meat, and onions until all the meat and vegetables are in the pot. Take care to end with a layer of potatoes. Fill the casserole to the top with wine, dot the surface with the chopped butter, and cook, covered, in a 350° oven for three hours, or until the meat is tender. Remove surface fat before serving.

RICE WITH ZUCCHINI

Rice combined with peas is a familiar mixture, but as a companion to seafood—shrimp, for example—I prefer rice with chopped, sautéed zucchini.

INGREDIENTS FOR SIX CUPS OF COOKED RICE

3 medium zucchini

3 Tbsp olive oil

pinch of saffron

salt and pepper

1 Tbsp parsley, very finely chopped

1 clove garlic (optional)

To make: Wash zucchini and trim ends, but do not peel. Cut them into quarters lengthwise, and cut out and discard the pulpy interiors, leaving from one-half to three-fourth inch of the firm outer parts. Slice or chop into pieces somewhat larger than a large pea. Heat the oil in a shallow frying pan. (If you like garlic, sauté a clove gently in the oil for two minutes. Remove before adding zucchini.) Add the chopped zucchini, and cook over fairly high heat, stirring and turning the pieces constantly with a spatula until they begin to brown. Turn down heat, add the saffron, and cook until the zucchini is just tender, continuing the turning and stirring. When the zucchini pieces are done, the texture of the vegetable should be similar to that of Chinese cooked vegetables. Add the salt, pepper, and chopped parsley.

To serve: Either mix the zucchini into the rice or use it as a garnish to cover the surface of the rice.

A DISH FOR THOSE WHO LIKE CABBAGE

I don't suggest serving this to guests unless you are certain of their tastes. Many people just don't like cabbage or, as they are so fond of saying, it doesn't like them. No matter, cook it up and eat it in secret if you must; if you like cabbage, it is worth being furtive about. And don't forget, if you cook cabbage properly over low heat, you can avoid its telltale aroma.

INGREDIENTS FOR TWO

¾ lb Canadian bacon, sliced (Because of its mildness, the genuine imported article is best, but any other good-quality bacon of the same cut will do. In a pinch, slices of mild boiled ham will do.)

1 small head green cabbage (trimmed of the outside leaves and coarse core), quartered

8 small new potatoes

2 Tbsp butter

1 tsp fresh dill, very finely chopped, or dried dill weed, pulverized (optional)

salt and pepper

1 tsp parsley, very, very finely chopped (optional)

To make: Peel the potatoes and put them on to boil. After ten minutes, begin steaming the cabbage. An ideal steamer is a wire colander with a trivet base (to hold the colander proper a few inches above the water).

Put one and one-half inches of water in a large pot and bring it to a boil. Put the colander in the pot, add the quartered cabbage, cover the pot with aluminum foil, and cook over medium heat for ten minutes or until tender. While this is going on, sauté the bacon in the butter until lightly browned, turning the slices once. Keep hot.

To serve: On a platter arrange the cabbage, potatoes, and bacon. Add salt and pepper to the cabbage and potatoes and, if you decide to use it, the dill. Pour the bacon pan juices on the cabbage. If you like, add butter to the potatoes and sprinkle them with the chopped parsley.

SZEKELY GULYAS

*Szekely gulya*s is a famous Hungarian goulash (the Viennese, of course, have their version). Like all famous dishes it has many partisans, and every partisan assumes he is the only one who knows how to make it. In fact, some of the most vociferous partisans of this dish don't even make it, they just get excited about it. Most of the bickering centers on whether or not tomatoes should be used. When I pointed out to an anti-tomato partisan that an ex-president of Hungary in exile in the United States had served *Szekely gulyas* to his guests at a press party and that the recipe he used, which was printed in a newspaper report of the affair, included tomatoes, his response was typical: he mumbled something to the effect that living in Jersey did things to people. For my part, if you like a dish prepared a certain way, by all means eat it that way— I don't have the missionary impulse.

Taking the above with a grain of salt, I recommend this recipe. It is particularly useful as a buffet dish; it can be eaten with a fork and, while substantial enough, it is not really heavy. While I have recommended noodles, preferably homemade, as an accompaniment, new potatoes also go very well with this goulash. Incidentally, *Szekely gulyas* is even better when reheated, and it freezes well.

INGREDIENTS FOR SIX

1 large onion, chopped

3 Tbsp butter

1 green pepper, chopped

5 medium tomatoes, peeled and seeded

½ lb veal, cut in strips

½ lb tender beef, cut in strips

½ lb pork, cut in strips (Remove excess fat from the meat.)

2½ tsp salt

6 peppercorns

2 bay leaves

½ tsp capers

1 tsp caraway seeds

1 Tbsp paprika

½ cup beef or chicken stock

1½ lb sauerkraut, drained

1½ cups sour cream

To make: Sauté the onion in butter until very soft but not brown and then add the tomatoes and green pepper. Cook for about fifteen minutes over very low heat, then

[181]

add the meat, salt, peppercorns, bay leaves, capers, caraway seeds, and paprika. Add the stock and simmer, covered, for thirty minutes. Then add the sauerkraut and cook for one hour longer. Serve the sour cream separately.

To serve: Serve with noodles (see p. 11) or boiled potatoes on the side.

STUFFED CABBAGE

Stuffed cabbage has surely crossed more national borders than any other dish. It can be found in Turkey (the Turks probably invented it), Greece, and the entire Middle East as well as North Africa, all the Slavic countries, Germany, Austria, Hungary, and Rumania. It even turns up as the specialty of Grasse, a charming sleepy French town situated above Cannes that functions as the world center of the preparation of flower essences used in the manufacture of perfumes —a fact that ought to give thought to those citizens who object to the odor of cooking cabbage. It is true that in Turkey and Greece vine leaves are more often stuffed, that in Russia krauted cabbage leaves are frequently used, and that in Grasse the whole cabbage is stuffed and held together in a special sort of string bag called a *sou fassum*. But essentially these are all versions of the same idea, and with such a background the dish obviously has merit.

The following is my recipe and the only point I would emphasize is that the rice be mixed into the stuffing uncooked. This does more than assure a good texture for the filling; it produces, through the swelling of the rice during the cooking, a plump finished product.

INGREDIENTS FOR FOUR TO SIX

1 large head of green cabbage

½ lb lean veal, ground

½ lb lean beef, ground

1 large onion, finely chopped (for the filling)

1 medium onion, finely chopped (for the sauce)

2 ounces dried mushrooms, preferably Polish, simmered in bouillon for thirty minutes (optional)

1 cup uncooked rice, washed well

½ cup dry white wine

3 cups beef or chicken stock, or more

1 large (28-ounce) can tomatoes

3 Tbsp fresh dill, chopped, or dried dill weed, to taste (about 1 tsp)

⅛ tsp leaf thyme

1 large bay leaf

salt and pepper

To make: To prepare the cabbage leaves, with a sharp, stout knife, remove and reject the core of the cabbage. Remove and discard all imperfect or discolored leaves. Carefully separate the leaves one by one and blanch them, three or four at a time, in a large pot of boiling water until they are limp. Drain the leaves in a colander. (If the cabbage is very firm so that the leaves are too tight to remove in the fashion described above, put the whole head of cabbage in the boiling water and remove after ten minutes, using a sturdy, long-handled kitchen fork thrust in the core of the cabbage. Drain, cool, and remove as many leaves as will readily

[1 8 3]

separate from the head. Repeat this process until all suitable leaves are separated.) With a knife remove and reject the thick, hard part of each leaf which extends about one-third of the way from the core end. Stack the leaves in a pile, convex-side up to permit them to drain.

To prepare the filling: Sauté the chopped onion until transparent, but not browned. Add the ground veal and beef and continue cooking until the meat has changed color. Add the mushrooms and the mushroom liquid, mix in the well-washed rice, and set aside. If you don't use the mushrooms, add one-half cup of bouillon instead.

To prepare the sauce: Sauté the chopped onion until transparent, and add the tomatoes, white wine, dill, thyme, bay leaf, and three cups of bouillon. Simmer for thirty minutes over low heat, then add salt and pepper to taste.

Preheat the oven to 350°. Turn the leaves over so that the concave side is up. Put a tablespoon of the filling mixture on each leaf and roll up like a package, turning in the ends. Place the rolls in an earthenware or glass dish with the seams down. Fit the rolls in close together without pressing and all in one layer. Pour the sauce over the rolls, cover with aluminum foil, and cook in a 350° oven for one hour and thirty minutes. After thirty minutes, and again after one hour, check the liquid in the dish. If it is considerably reduced, add bouillon or water.

Note: Another method of cooking the cabbage rolls is to brown them in a metal skillet or roasting pan in butter or oil before adding the sauce. The flavor is slightly different, and I like it. Unless they are browned on one side only, the rolls have to be tied.

To serve: Stuffed cabbage may be served hot or cold. If served cold, garnish with slices of lemon. Sour cream goes well with stuffed cabbage, hot or cold.

Miniature cabbage rolls make a good hors d'oeuvre served with glasses of chilled vodka. If desired, omit the tomatoes from the sauce and use more bouillon and white wine. Try flavoring the vodka with caraway seeds.

VEGETABLES

ELSEWHERE in this book I have complained about the way restaurants treat vegetables. In justice, I should say that there are very good reasons why vegetables fare so poorly in a commercial context. In the first place, unless a restaurant is one of those exceedingly rare and very, very expensive establishments that cook everything to order, the problem of how to serve vegetables that do not look and taste like leftovers is always present. As anyone experienced in vegetable cookery has observed, a batch of green beans, say, that has been cooked *à point* (just right) remains *à point* for a minute or so, but after that the bloom vanishes and the beans look and taste like leftovers. This is where home cooking has the edge on restaurants: you know what you are going to cook, how many people you are cooking for, and can time the cooking so that vegetables keep that elusive bloom of freshness.

STUFFED COOKED TOMATOES

One of the most attractive garnishes is a stuffed tomato —that is, a tomato that has been carefully selected, properly prepared for stuffing, and, needless to say, stuffed with something appropriate. For instance, a tomato stuffed with broccoli in a *béchamel* sauce would go very well with a mutton chop, just as obviously as it would not go with poached fish. What sort of stuffed tomato would go with a piece of poached fish? Try a tomato stuffed with sorrel or creamed spinach. Do not use very large tomatoes for stuffing: they tend to split before they are done. Use tomatoes that are just ripe, neither too soft nor too hard.

To be stuffed and baked, tomatoes must, in addition to being emptied of their interior pulp and seeds, be drained of some of the watery juice retained in the flesh. This is easily done by salting their interiors and turning them upside down in a dish. After twenty minutes or so a good deal of water will have drained into the dish, and the tomatoes will be ready for stuffing and baking. If you stuffed tomatoes not drained in this way—say, with a puree of green beans—the sauce would be very thin on the bottom, and the tomatoes would probably split. In addition, the flavor would be excessively acid.

[187]

Because it is quite thin, the shell of a tomato doesn't take long to cook—about twenty minutes in a 350° oven, which is also sufficient time to thoroughly heat the precooked filling. In any case, keep an eye on the tomatoes as they cook and test them by prodding with your finger.

Here is a list of a few of the vegetables best suited for stuffing tomatoes that are to be used as a garnish. For the most part, it is advisable to puree or chop the vegetables to be used for stuffing; and pureed and chopped vegetables are best when mixed with a sauce or with cream. The most useful sauces for this are *béchamel* (see p. 22) and *Mornay* (see p. 24). If you can get very small peas, use them whole, with or without a sauce. Add a little butter to the peas before filling the tomato if you are not using a sauce. If pea-stuffed tomatoes are served with lamb, add a little chopped mint.

Note: The proportion of sauce to vegetable in the following recipes should be one-half cup sauce to two cups vegetable, which, when mixed, provides enough stuffing to fill from six to seven tomatoes, depending on their size.

Broccoli: Poach or steam, chop finely, and mix with *Mornay* sauce. Serve with roast pork, roast beef, leg of lamb, or lamb chops.

Green beans: Boil, chop or puree, and mix with *béchamel* sauce. Serve with roast beef, roast chicken, or roast veal.

Brussels sprouts: Cook, chop finely, and mix with a *béchamel* sauce made with beef stock. Serve with roast beef and Yorkshire pudding.

Green peas: If small enough, serve whole. Otherwise puree in a blender (it purees the skins, which is desirable) and mix with *béchamel* sauce. This goes well with just about everything.

Eggplant: Put the whole eggplant under the broiler and grill it until it is quite soft, turning from time to time. Slash the skin, scoop out the pulp, and put it into a glass or stainless steel bowl. Reject the skin. Add two tablespoons of olive oil, salt, pepper, and a pinch of leaf thyme. Mash into a puree. Serve with roast leg of lamb or roast veal.

Cauliflower: Poach in salted water until tender, chop, and mix with *béchamel* sauce or *Mornay* sauce. Serve with fresh ham or roast loin of pork.

Zucchini: Do not peel. If the zucchini are large, remove and reject the soft inner parts with the seeds. Chop into pieces the size of a pea and sauté in olive oil, with or without garlic. A sauce is not necessary.

Another method is to boil the zucchini and puree. Mix in a little olive oil or butter and a little heavy cream, as well as a pinch of thyme and a pinch of cayenne pepper. If the puree is not stiff enough, reduce the liquid in the puree by cooking it over medium heat, stirring constantly. Serve with roast beef, leg of lamb, roast pork, ham, or roast chicken.

Mushrooms: Clean, chop, and sauté in butter. Add a little lemon juice and a pinch of cayenne pepper. This goes well with all roast meats, chops, and grilled or baked fish.

If you wish, puree the mushrooms in a blender and mix with a little cream. This goes well with just about everything, but is especially good with fish.

Sorrel: Clean and sauté without adding any more water than is left on the leaves after cleaning. Mix with a *béchamel* sauce. Serve with fish. (Sorrel requires very little cooking; when the leaves begin to "melt," it is done.)

Spinach: Use frozen chopped spinach. Mix with a *béchamel* or *Mornay* sauce, or with sour cream and one-eighth teaspoon grated nutmeg. Serve with veal scallops, fish, lamb, chicken, or ham.

FRESH (GREEN) CORN

There are four essentials for corn on the cob: it must be very fresh; nothing in the way of other foods should be allowed to interfere with its consumption; there must be a great deal of it on hand, cooked in successive batches; and it should be served with its natural complements of butter, salt, and pepper, freshly ground. Corn (like asparagus, like oysters, like *soupe au pistou*) seems to produce a gustatory enthusiasm that overwhelms any notion of normal capacities, and it inspires a fixedness of purpose that makes a shambles of anything resembling a structured meal into which one attempts to fit it. The best thing, then, is to give way to the inevitable and enjoy the corn.

To make: Remove the husks and the silk and cook the corn in unsalted boiling water for five minutes. Actually, a few minutes suffice, but I am taking into consideration the time it takes for the water to boil again after the corn has been added. Cook it in batches in a rhythm that keeps the guests supplied. Have a large receptacle on hand for the demolished cobs.

To serve: The only other food I can think of that would fit into this strictly American feast is Smithfield ham, sliced paper-thin, with some hot biscuits. The logical drink is chilled dry white wine or whiskey. (This certainly is not an occasion to which the irritating instruction—in the past so common in American cookbooks, especially Southern ones—"serve plenty of hot coffee" applies. I don't believe that instruction was ever necessary, since I have yet to read a recipe that concluded with the advice to serve niggardly portions of tepid coffee.) For dessert I can't think of anything better than a plain apple tart, after which strong coffee, in quantities dictated by demand, would be welcome.

SAUTÉED SNOW PEAS

If you can buy fine fresh snow peas (usually available in Chinese shops in the larger cities), do so. I have bought frozen snow peas imported from Taiwan which are as good as I have ever eaten. Oddly enough, although an identical pea is widely sold in Paris under the name *mange-tout* (eat all), in the years I lived there I never saw them on a restaurant menu or was served them in a French home. I can only assume that at least some French—and it would be characteristically French—bought the peas out of curiosity. It also occurred to me that—since there were, and are, a good many French in Paris who have lived in the Far East, especially in what used to be called Indochina—some bought them to use in Oriental dishes. The method of cooking in this recipe preserves the crispness of the vegetable, as is the Chinese fashion.

INGREDIENTS FOR FOUR

1 lb snow peas

½ cup water

½ tsp salt

⅛ tsp pepper

juice of ¼ medium lemon

2 Tbsp butter

To make: Put the water into a skillet, add the snow peas, and bring to a boil. Turn the heat down and, as if you were sautéing them in butter or oil, stir the peas frequently until they are tender, but still crisp—from eight to ten minutes. Drain them, add the salt, pepper, lemon juice, and butter, and stir well. Serve immediately.

Note: I sometimes chop the peas or cut them *en julienne* (in thin strips) and serve them as a garnish for steamed rice. Cook them precisely as above, but they will take less time. Sprinkle them over the surface of a dish of rice, or mix them into the rice. A few chopped, uncooked chives are a nice additional touch.

SPINACH

The French sometimes have quirks and fixations about vegetables. In the case of spinach, they feel that you must wash it in one vessel of water and cook it in another. This subdues the spinach. But even that isn't enough; they then chop it up. This recipe goes well with ham, veal scallops, roast beef, and countless other dishes, including fish.

INGREDIENTS FOR FOUR

2 lb fresh spinach

⅛ tsp nutmeg, or a little more

1 cup sour cream, at room temperature

1 clove garlic, very, very finely chopped (optional)

salt and pepper

To make: Remove the stems of the spinach and the yellowed bits of the leaves. Wash it in a large pot, agitating it so that any sand or grit will settle to the bottom. Remove from the water by handfuls and drain in a colander, pressing to eliminate as much water as possible. Then put the spinach in a large pot and forget about it for about fifteen minutes. More water will settle to the bottom during this time. Pour it off. Now begin cooking the spinach over the lowest possible heat, with the pot covered. (The water clinging to the leaves after draining will provide enough moisture to cook the spinach; in fact, this is the key to spinach cookery.)

If you decide to use the garlic, add it before covering the pot and mix it in well. When the spinach leaves have wilted, add the nutmeg, salt, and pepper. Mix thoroughly. Cook for ten minutes, then add the sour cream. Mix it into the spinach and, when the cream is just heated, serve.

SAUERKRAUT

This sauerkraut is not the fat, smoked-meat flavored version, which has its merits, but usually turns out to be a once-a-year winter dish. Actually sauerkraut can be refreshing instead of heavy, as I think this recipe proves.

INGREDIENTS FOR FOUR OR FIVE

2 lb sauerkraut

1 large onion, finely chopped

2 Tbsp butter

2 bay leaves

1 tsp cumin, ground, or 1 Tbsp caraway seeds (optional)

dry white wine, enough to cover

chicken or beef bouillon, enough to cover

pepper

To make: Wash and drain the sauerkraut only if it has a strong odor. Pull it with a fork to loosen it. Sauté the onion in butter, but do not brown. Add the sauerkraut, bay leaves, pepper, the ground cumin or the caraway seeds, and equal amounts of wine and bouillon to cover the sauerkraut well. Stir very well, bring to a boil, reduce the heat to very low, cover, and cook for at least two hours—three hours is better. Add more wine and stock as the liquid in the pot reduces. Although they are optional, I like the cumin or caraway seeds because they add a mild pungency to an essentially bland dish.

To serve: Try serving sauerkraut with a roasted fresh ham or a loin of pork, accompanied by boiled potatoes, applesauce, and pan gravy.

Note: In Alsace, juniper berries are traditionally used to spice sauerkraut. If you like the flavor (which goes well with game birds—pheasant, for example), use them, but omit the cumin or caraway seeds. Use only five or six juniper berries; they are quite pungent.

If you like a creamy sauerkraut, grate a large raw potato into the sauerkraut mixture forty-five minutes before it is done.

KASHA

If you are not familiar with *kasha*, a middle- and eastern-European staple, I urge you to try it. It is not difficult to make, it is flavorful, and it is high in protein. *Kasha* goes particularly well with roast pork, shashlik, grilled chicken, and roast leg of lamb. In Vienna and other middle-European cities and towns, *kasha* is used as a filling for a non-dessert strudel, in which case it is cooked in meat stock and flavored with onions, mushrooms, and herbs—a procedure perfectly applicable to *kasha* served as a side dish. Like rice, *kasha* marries well with a variety of ingredients, but above all it comes into its own when served with one tablespoon or more of sour cream per serving.

INGREDIENTS FOR SIX

1½ cups kasha

3 cups beef or chicken stock

2 small eggs

salt and pepper

4 Tbsp butter or sour cream

To make: Beat the eggs lightly and mix them into the *kasha.* Put the mixture into a heavy skillet over high heat. Stir, scrape, and toss until each grain is separate, breaking up lumps and clusters with a fork. Transfer the *kasha* to a two-quart pot that has been well heated. Bring the stock to a boil and add it to the pot. Turn down the heat to low, cover the pot, and allow the mixture to cook for thirty minutes.

To serve: Add salt and pepper and a generous amount of butter, or pass sour cream. A nice variation is to add (for the amount of *kasha* the above recipe produces), just before serving, one bunch of scallions with one-third of the green parts, finely chopped and sautéed in butter, or a mixture of one bunch of scallions and one cup of mushrooms, finely chopped and sautéed.

CARROTS BURGUNDY STYLE

Carrots cooked Burgundy style are a fitting side dish to *boeuf bourguignon,* braised beef, pot roast, *carbonnades de boeuf,* or any other stewed or braised beef dish. This method of preparation makes it easy to time their cooking, so that the carrots can arrive at the table hot the moment the main dish is served.

*2 lb carrots (the younger, the better), scraped,
cut in quarters lengthwise, and halved crosswise
(If available, use whole small carrots.)*

1 Tbsp butter

1 Tbsp olive oil

salt and pepper

parsley, very finely chopped (optional)

To make: Cook the carrots in salted water until almost
done. Drain them and set aside until about ten minutes
before time to serve. At that time, heat the butter and
oil in a frying pan. When the butter and oil are hot,
but not smoking, add the carrots, turn the heat down,
and sauté until they are nicely browned on all sides.
Turn them often. When done, dry the carrots quickly
on paper towels and sprinkle well with salt and pepper.

Note: Do not prolong the sautéing, or the carrots are
likely to become soggy and limp.

To serve: If you wish, serve with a light sprinkling of
very finely chopped parsley.

CARROTS WITH TARRAGON

Fresh tarragon is hard to come by, but we do have
excellent dried tarragon in the United States. Unfortunately, like dried basil, it has a tendency to turn an
unappetizing dark color when cooked, but one can ex-
ploit the good flavor while dodging the substance.

INGREDIENTS FOR SIX

2 lb young carrots, peeled or scraped and cut into strips or slices

2 cups beef or chicken stock

1 Tbsp dried tarragon

2 Tbsp butter

salt (very little; the stock is salty) and pepper

juice of ½ lemon

To make: Cook the stock with the tarragon, salt, pepper, and lemon juice for fifteen minutes. Strain the mixture into the pot in which you intend to cook the carrots. Add the carrots and the butter, cover the pot, and cook until the liquid has been almost completely absorbed. The carrots will be soft, but very flavorful.

Note: If you wish to stuff artichoke hearts with carrots cooked in this fashion, chop the carrots up before cooking them, and, when they are done, mix in a little heavy cream and one tablespoon of very, very finely chopped parsley.

SALAD WITH BACON AND VINEGAR DRESSING

Salad with bacon and vinegar dressing is usually associated with German cookery, but actually it originates, or extends, somewhat to the south in the region of Rheims in the Champagne country of France. It ends, or begins, somewhere in the middle of Russia. This salad is the northern response to uncooked greens, which are accommodated so easily in the southern countries by olive oil. Bacon and vinegar dressing has its merits. It can make iceberg head lettuce taste delicious—no small accomplishment—and its peculiar sweet-sour sharpness is ideal when served with roast chicken, roast pork, or cold meats. With this dressing, it is best to chop the greens rather finely.

INGREDIENTS FOR FOUR

6 slices lean bacon, finely chopped

1 small head of iceberg lettuce, finely shredded

4 Tbsp wine vinegar

1 tsp white granulated sugar

salt and pepper

To make: Sauté the bacon in a skillet until it has rendered most of its fat and is crisp. Pour off and reject half of the fat, add the sugar, and cook until it begins to carmelize. Turn down the heat, add the vinegar (this causes a minor explosion), and stir and scrape until the mixture is amalgamated. Pour it over the lettuce, add salt and pepper, mix well, and serve.

Note: It is with this recipe that one makes wilted salad. A tender lettuce, such as Simpson or leaf which will wilt at the slightest touch of heat, is substituted for the iceberg above. Wash and dry the lettuce, add the hot dressing, and stir and mix well. The wilting process can be assisted by heating the salad bowl (do not use a wooden one) in hot water.

CURRIED PEAS AND CAULIFLOWER

Curried peas and cauliflower is an unusual combination that transforms ordinary ingredients into a triumph. I serve it with a plain lamb or chicken curry, without peanuts or chopped bacon as condiments.

INGREDIENTS FOR FOUR

1 small head of firm white cauliflower or 2 packages frozen cauliflower

1 package frozen peas

1 medium onion, peeled and finely chopped

3 Tbsp butter or 2 Tbsp butter and 1 Tbsp oil

1 to 2 Tbsp good-quality curry powder or the same amount of cumin, ground, and tumeric, powdered

1 clove garlic, peeled and finely chopped

salt and pepper

To make: Heat the butter or butter and oil, and sauté the chopped onion and garlic for one minute or two, stirring constantly with a wooden spoon. Add the curry powder and cook for four minutes over the lowest heat, stirring constantly. It is necessary to cook the curry powder before adding liquid, but take care not to burn it. Now add the fresh cauliflower, broken into segments, or the frozen cauliflower, separated with a fork. Mix and toss thoroughly so that some of the butter-curry powder mixture is on each segment. Then add one cup of hot water, cover the pot, and turn down the heat to very low. Add more water if the cauliflower begins to stick to the bottom of the pot. Cook until the cauliflower is almost done, then add the peas. Mix well, cover the pot again, and cook until the peas are tender. Add salt and pepper and mix thoroughly just before serving.

Note: If you like peppery hot food, add a dash of cayenne pepper or, better yet, green chili peppers— fresh, if you can buy them, or canned, which can be found in the Mexican foods section in most super-markets.

To serve: This dish goes with rice as if it were made for it and is particularly good with shrimp and rice dishes.

SPECIAL FRIED POTATOES

Serve these special fried potatoes with really-first class steaks. Although a bit of trouble, they are worth it.

INGREDIENTS FOR FOUR

4 large (not monstrous) Idaho potatoes, peeled and cut up as for French fries (Each piece should be more than twice the size of an ordinary French-fried potato; six pieces per large potato would be just right. They should be cut the full length of the potatoes.)

oil

To make: Cook the pieces of potato in boiling water for six minutes. Drain them and allow to dry. Oil a very large, flat skillet or two smaller ones and gently sauté the pieces, turning them until they are brown on all sides. Use just enough oil to prevent scorching. Raise and lower the heat as required. The result should be a sublimated fried potato, uniformly fondant and uniformly crisp.

To serve: It may sound like shades of fish and chips, but try the potatoes sprinkled with a few drops of white wine vinegar and a lot of salt and pepper.

[201]

ARTICHOKES

If vegetables were graded into classes, the artichoke would certainly rate the blue ribbon. As a vegetable it has everything—flavor, texture, digestibility—and it is nourishing without being fattening. Its only flaw, and it is a flaw only to the inexperienced, is that it is somewhat difficult to handle. However, with a stout knife with a serrated blade (for example, a bread knife) and a small, sharp knife, you can clean and prepare artichokes for cooking in any of a number of fashions in just a few minutes. If you don't have a knife with a serrated blade, a pair of kitchen scissors will do equally well.

There are three standard ways of preparing artichokes for cooking:

WHOLE: Remove and reject any coarse or discolored outside leaves. Cut off the stem flush with the artichoke bottom. Cut off and reject one-third of the tops of the leaves.

QUARTERED: Prepare as above, but cut into quarters and remove the furry choke part above the heart, using a sharp knife.

HEARTS: Cut off the stem and with a sharp knife remove all the green leafy parts, but leave the choke (which is easily removed after the heart is cooked).

Since all the leaves of an artichoke grow from the heart—the tender part—trim away only the green, obviously tough parts around the heart, which in its uncooked state is cream colored.

When cleaning artichokes, have a halved lemon at hand to rub on the cut surfaces of the vegetable to prevent discoloration. Another method is to add lemon juice or white vinegar to a bowl of water, immersing the artichoke from time to time as you work.

WHOLE BOILED ARTICHOKES

Boiling is the easiest way to cook artichokes and perhaps the best. The flavor of boiled artichokes, like that of asparagus, is enhanced by a hollandaise sauce (see p. 30) when served hot and by a vinaigrette sauce (see p. 29) when served cold. But however you serve them, whole artichokes should be a separate course. To do justice to a good-sized whole artichoke demands application and a certain amount of time.

INGREDIENTS FOR FOUR

4 large or medium artichokes, cleaned (see p. 202)

juice of 1 medium lemon or 2 Tbsp white vinegar

salt

parsley, very finely chopped

To make: Choose a pot that will just hold the artichokes placed side by side. However, before putting the artichokes in the pot, bring sufficient water to cover the artichokes to a boil. Add the lemon juice or vinegar, the salt, and then the artichokes, stem ends down. Cook until tender, but not mushy. Test after twenty minutes by pulling out a large leaf from one of the artichokes. If it comes out easily and the heart end is tender, the artichokes are done. Another test is to turn an artichoke over and plunge a toothpick in the center.

To serve: If the artichokes are to be served hot, take them out of the pot and place them stem end up on a plate and allow them to drain for a few minutes. If they are to be served cold, drain them in the same fashion, but allow them to cool. Spread the leaves apart and remove the chokes with the tip of a spoon. Sprinkle a little very finely chopped parsley in the interior of each artichoke.

QUARTERED AND SAUTÉED ARTICHOKES

Cooked in this fashion, artichokes go with grilled lamb, roast beef, scallops of veal, and grilled fish. A distinct advantage of this preparation is that, should the meal be held up, it may be kept warm for some time without losing its bloom.

INGREDIENTS FOR FOUR

4 medium or 6 small artichokes

2 Tbsp olive oil

juice of 1 medium lemon

½ tsp dried oregano

1 tsp parsley, very finely chopped

salt and pepper

1 clove garlic, finely chopped (optional)

butter (optional)

To make: Clean and quarter the artichokes (see p. 202). To a heavy-bottomed pan or pot, large enough to accommodate the artichoke quarters without crowding, add the oil, lemon juice, oregano, garlic, and artichokes. Sauté for five minutes, then add one cup of water. Cover the pan and cook over low heat until the liquid has been all but completely reduced and absorbed. Turn the quarters over during the cooking, and test with a toothpick after fifteen minutes. As always with artichokes, the pieces should not be too soft. The addition of a finely chopped clove of garlic won't hurt.

To serve: Add salt, pepper, parsley, and a little butter if you wish. Mix well and serve.

This recipe can be varied in any of the following ways:

Use the same quantity of dried tarragon instead of dried oregano.

Use chicken or beef bouillon instead of water.

Use three tomatoes, peeled, seeded, and chopped, with one-fourth cup water or bouillon.

Omit the oregano and add two tablespoons fresh basil when the artichokes are just done.

Use a pinch of thyme and one-half teaspoon dried basil instead of the oregano.

Prepare in any of the above fashions and mix with boiled, quartered new potatoes. Just before serving, mix in one tablespoon butter.

Prepare in any of the above fashions and mix with very small peas, cooked separately with a pinch of mint.

Prepare in any of the above fashions, but add at the beginning five or six finely chopped scallions with some of the green part.

Prepare in any of the above fashions (but preferably with chicken or beef bouillon) and mix in, before serving, one tablespoon very finely slivered ham, preferably Italian Prosciutto or Westphalian ham.

Prepare in any of the above fashions and, just before serving, sprinkle with fine white bread crumbs fried in butter.

If you don't like herbs, sauté the quartered artichokes without the oregano and, just before serving, mix in one cup of good *béchamel* sauce (see p. 22).

ARTICHOKE HEARTS

An artichoke heart is an artichoke divested of its leaves and choke and then trimmed to form a perfectly symmetrical, spherical, solid piece of vegetable elegance that, as a garnish, needs to defer in class only to truffles and *morilles*. This being so, and a glance at any first-class French cookbook will back me up, why is it that artichoke hearts do not figure as even an infrequent part of the American diet? The answer, I am afraid, is that they demand a little work and a certain amount of skill to prepare. More to the point, they do not fit easily into a culinary tradition that relegates the vegetable to an inconsequential substance that appears with meat. This makes a certain amount of sense; if you are going to spoil vegetables, why bother with something as troublesome as artichokes?

Having vented my spleen, let me say that I realize that there is more to the problem of cooking vegetables than laziness and carelessness, I would attribute most bad cooking to a lack of confidence, which turns up as a lack of motivation, or vice versa. My plea—and it is a plea—is to cook vegetables so that they are a triumph rather than a left-handed stint offered in the name of that much abused deity—nutrition.

The artichoke on the left in the top photograph is ready for paring to produce a heart as shown on the right. The artichoke second from the left has been cut in half to indicate the position of the heart: at the very bottom of the vegetable. The French term for an artichoke heart, fond d'artichaut, *translates literally as "the bottom of an artichoke."*

The bottom photograph shows poached eggs with hearts of artichokes. The sauce is rouille, *the sprigs are parsley.*

To make: Prepare the hearts (see p. 202) and cook them in water to which salt has been added and (for a two-quart pot) the juice of one small lemon. Test the hearts with a fork after fifteen minutes. They will probably take longer than that to cook, but they should not be mushy.

Because of their shape—concave on one side, convex on the other—artichoke hearts almost demand a filling, although they may be sliced and served with butter, parsley, and slices of lemon. The ideal fillings are very small peas, a puree of fresh peas, minuscule carrots, poached scallions (only the white parts), chopped mushrooms, a puree of mushrooms, a puree of spinach, and just about any other vegetable except yellow turnips and cabbage.

To serve: Artichoke hearts may be served with chilled poached eggs and a *Béarnaise* sauce, or mayonnaise, or—and particularly fine—with *foie gras* and port wine-flavored aspic.

BEETS

The only beets I would consider serving are freshly cooked ones. To cook beets, leave at least three inches of the beet stems and do not remove the spindly bottom of the root. Do not peel, but wash if the beets need it. Put them into a large pot of cold water, bring the water to a boil, turn down the heat, and cook until tender, which will take about one hour, or more, depending on the size of the beets. As with all vegetables cooked in water or baked, it is desirable that they be of uniform size. When they are done, drain the beets in a colander and allow them to cool enough to be handled. Peel them by slipping off the skins with your fingers. Then trim off the ends.

Note: If, by chance, the green tops of fresh beets are in good condition, clean them as you would spinach and cook with only the water left on the leaves after washing. Cook over low heat until tender, which shouldn't take more than fifteen minutes. Flavor with salt, pepper, butter, and a few drops of lemon juice.

Following are six ways of preparing beets. One recipe is for a hot beet dish and five are for salads. Note that the abominable concoction known as Harvard beets is not included.

PLAIN BEET SALAD

Beet salads are very versatile. They can serve as a light *hors d'oeuvre*, as part of an *hors d'oeuvre varié*, and are never out of place on the table when turkey, duck, goose, or pork is served. Salads made with beets (except when combined with greens that tend to wilt) generally should be made and chilled in the refrigerator at least two hours in advance of serving. Put the salad on a lower shelf in the refrigerator, where it will chill but not freeze.

INGREDIENTS FOR FOUR

4 medium beets, cooked as above (For proper amalgamation of flavors, the beets should be warm when mixed with the other ingredients.)

5 Tbsp olive oil

2 Tbsp red wine vinegar

1 Tbsp parsley, very, very finely chopped

salt and pepper

To make: Slice the beets into a glass or porcelain bowl. Mix all the other ingredients and pour the mixture over the beets. Mix all together very well with two wooden spoons, but do it lightly—beets are fragile enough. Chill the salad in the refrigerator for at least two hours before serving.

SALAD OF BEETS AND CELERY

I consider this combination just about perfect. Both the textures and the flavors of the two vegetables, while very different, complement each other perfectly. It is a good salad to serve after a sauced dish, and it can be served with a course consisting of any sort of game —rather like cranberries with turkey. Salad of beets and celery goes particularly well with roast pheasant.

INGREDIENTS FOR FOUR

4 medium beets, cooked as above, sliced in julienne strips (the shape of a kitchen match, but twice as thick)

1½ cups celery heart, properly cleaned and devoid of the coarse fibers (Pare the stalks on the top surface, break them to determine which fibers remain, remove, and reject. The celery should then be cut into julienne strips, as the beets.)

5 Tbsp olive oil

2 Tbsp red wine vinegar

¼ tsp Dijon mustard

salt and pepper

To make: In a glass or porcelain bowl, mix the oil, vinegar, mustard, salt, and pepper. Add the beets and celery and mix lightly, but well. Chill in the refrigerator for at least two hours before serving.

BEET SALAD WITH SOUR CREAM DRESSING

Anyone familiar with Polish or Russian cooking is aware that beets and sour cream have a strong affinity. *Borstch*, which is based on the beet, is a good example. But Americans must wonder why the Slavs in general seem fixated on winter vegetables, such as cabbage, beets, potatoes, turnips, and pickles. The answer is very simple. The Slavic world (despite the fact that it seems to be progressing by leaps and bounds—in the wrong directions, of course) still does not have anything resembling our distribution system, which provides an immense variety of greens, *fresh* root vegetables (beets, for example), and fruit the year round. In other words, the masters of the countries on the other side of the iron curtain do not deem it important to make available to their citizens in the North what is easily produced in the southern provinces. It is ironic that the Russians, who put the first man in space, have not yet found a way to economically transport a Georgian apricot to Moscow. This situation, as we know, has led numerous Georgians and other Russian "southerners" in the winter to pack suitcases with small but valuable amounts of fruit, travel by air to Moscow or Leningrad, and sell without difficulty the contents of their suitcases at ghastly prices. This strikes me as a good example of a lop-sided economy, not to mention disregard of the ordinary Russian citizen, but I'll drop the subject; this is not a political book.

Beet salad with sour cream makes an excellent light hors d'oeuvre, but I should warn that it must be tart enough; beets and sour cream are bland and need a high proportion of lemon juice or vinegar to be appetizing. Another help is the addition of either chopped fresh dill or dried dill weed.

INGREDIENTS FOR FOUR

4 medium beets, cooked as above, chilled, trimmed, peeled, and sliced (For this salad, the beets should not be warm when mixed with the dressing.)

¾ cup sour cream

juice of 1 small lemon, strained, or 3 Tbsp red wine vinegar

1 heaping Tbsp fresh dill, finely chopped, or 1 tsp dried dill weed

salt and pepper

To make: Mix the sour cream with the lemon juice or vinegar; add the salt, pepper, and the dill. Lightly mix the beets with the sour cream mixture in a glass or porcelain serving dish. Chill or serve immediately.

Note: In each of the above beet salad recipes, one tablespoon of very finely chopped fresh chives adds a delicate sharpness without harshness.

BEETS WITH FIELD SALAD

Field salad, or *mâche* as it is known in France, is one of the most tender and flavorful salad greens. For some reason or other, it is very expensive in America, but I consider it worth the expense once in a while. Traditionally in France, field salad is served mixed with cooked beets and a vinaigrette sauce. The season for this delicious green starts at the end of summer and continues until winter sets in.

INGREDIENTS FOR FOUR

¾ lb field salad

3 medium beets, cooked as above and sliced

6 Tbsp olive oil

3 Tbsp red wine vinegar

salt and pepper

To make: Clean the field salad by trimming and rejecting the root ends of the clusters of leaves. Wash the leaves, drain, and shake dry in a towel (see p. 272). In a bowl, mix the leaves with the oil, add the beets, vinegar, salt, and pepper, and mix lightly but thoroughly. Serve immediately.

BEET SALAD WITH WATERCRESS

Although quite different in flavor from field salad, watercress combines well with beets, is generally available the year round, and is not expensive. The important factor in preparing watercress for salad is to remove and reject the stems, which are quite tough and fibrous. For this mixture, I prefer to cut the beets in julienne strips, but slightly larger than usual—about three times the thickness of a kitchen match. First slice the peeled and trimmed beets, then cut them into julienne strips.

[2 1 3]

INGREDIENTS FOR FOUR

1 bunch of watercress (the leaves only), washed, well drained, and dried

4 small beets, cooked, peeled, and cut into julienne strips

6 Tbsp olive oil

3 Tbsp red wine vinegar (This combination requires more vinegar than others.)

salt and pepper

To make: Mix the oil, vinegar, salt, and pepper until well blended. Add the beets and mix thoroughly. Chill in the refrigerator until just before serving. Then add the watercress leaves, mix well, and serve.

HOT BEETS WITH TARRAGON

INGREDIENTS FOR FOUR

4 medium beets, cooked as above, peeled, and sliced

2 Tbsp butter

¼ tsp dried leaf tarragon, pulverized by rubbing between the palms of your hands

salt and pepper

To make: Melt one tablespoon of butter in a pot, and over low heat warm the beets, tossing lightly. After three minutes, add the tarragon, salt, and pepper. When the beets are heated, add the other tablespoon of butter, chopped. Serve immediately.

ASPARAGUS

Whether to be served hot, tepid, or cold, the preparation of asparagus is always the same.

To make: Trim spears, retaining only the tender parts. To determine where the tender part begins, cut into the spears, starting one-third of their length from the bottom and continuing up until the knife blade cuts easily. Trim at that point. If the spears are quite short and very fresh, it isn't necessary to peel them, but it does make them more delicate. Peeling can be best done with a sharp knife, working down, but an ordinary potato peeler will also do the job.

Tie the asparagus, in a bunch or in bunches, two inches from the bottom and again just below the tips. If you have an asparagus boiler, you only have to pay attention to the timing. If you do not have a boiler, the asparagus can be cooked very well in any high-sided, not-too-wide pot. Heat three inches of water in the pot, place the bundle of asparagus upright in the water, and cover the top with a bowl, another pot, or an improvised cover of heavy aluminum foil. In any case, the bowl, pot, or foil cover should fit well enough to form a steamer. When the water starts to boil again, turn down the heat to medium. Do not overcook asparagus. Test with a sharp fork. If the tines of the fork meet moderate resistance just below the tips, the

[215]

asparagus are done. Lift them out by the strings and drain well before serving or adding sauce.

Fine, large asparagus is too good and too distinctive in flavor to be served as an accompaniment to other foods, although I would make an exception for that inspired German combination of Westphalian ham, chilled white asparagus, dark bread and butter, and white wine. Asparagus, when served either hot or cold as a separate course, demands a sauce worthy of it; and, for the most part, the sauces that complement asparagus in a solo role do not go well with other foods. For example, my wife and I were once served grilled fillet of beef with *sauce Béarnaise* and asparagus with hollandaise sauce—both on the same plate. This disaster was not the work of a professional, but what I regretted most about it was that the beef, the asparagus, and the sauces were all cooked to perfection. It was simply a case of "All that meat and no potatoes."

When serving asparagus cold, I would recommend one of the following sauces: mayonnaise (see p. 26), vinaigrette (see p. 29), or melted butter and lemon (except for the addition of salt and pepper, there is nothing more to this than the name implies).

To my mind, the best of all sauces for hot or warm asparagus is the simplest—melted butter, lemon, salt and pepper—although I do like hollandaise sauce (see p. 30) with asparagus, especially if the rest of the meal is not too heavy. Hot asparagus also goes well with orange sauce (see p. 31) and is excellent served *à la polonaise*. The most attractive way to present asparagus *à la polonaise* is to sprinkle crumbled hard-cooked egg yolks, chopped parsley, and sautéed bread crumbs over the tips and an inch or so down the stalks of the asparagus.

LIMA BEANS WITH GARLIC

Lima beans, particularly the small variety, have a good deal of the flavor and texture of that great French bean, the *flageolet*, which goes so well with leg of lamb. Try serving lima beans with roast pork, grilled lamb or pork chops, or grilled sausages.

INGREDIENTS FOR FOUR OR FIVE

2 packages frozen lima beans (the smallest variety)

1 clove garlic, crushed

1 Tbsp parsley, very finely chopped

2 Tbsp butter

salt and pepper

To make: Put the lima beans, garlic, salt, and pepper into a thick-bottomed pot, add three-fourths cup water, and cook over high heat until the beans have thawed and separated. Turn down the heat and simmer for twenty-five minutes, stirring lightly from time to time. If the mixture becomes too thick, add more hot water. Mix in the butter and parsley before serving. The beans should be meltingly soft and the sauce, creamy.

[2 1 7]

Note: As a variation, add two tablespoons of tomato paste when the beans have been set to simmer. If you like nutmeg or mace, add a pinch with the tomato paste.

ACORN SQUASH

As delicious as they are, I have always been irritated by the fact that baked acorn squash take up so much room on the plate. This cooking method is designed to eliminate that inconvenience.

INGREDIENTS FOR SIX

3 medium acorn squash

1 stick (¼ lb) butter

2 Tbsp oil

⅛ tsp leaf thyme

salt and white pepper

To make: Halve the squash and scoop out the seeds and membranes. Brush the squash with the oil and bake until they are soft. Allow to cool until they can be handled. Remove all the pulp from the shells and put it into a bowl. Mash the pulp until it is smooth and add salt, pepper, and thyme. Put into a shallow glass baking dish, and sprinkle the surface with ¼ of the butter, chopped into small pieces. Put the dish under the broiler and cook until the surface is nicely browned and crisp. Just before serving, break the surface crust and in each depression put a piece of the remaining butter.

[218]

To serve: Serve very hot. This acorn squash goes well with roast chicken, ham, pork, and especially with first-quality pork sausages.

GRILLED YELLOW (SUMMER) SQUASH

I can't think of a vegetable easier to prepare or more appreciated than grilled (broiled) summer squash, especially when it is served with roast chicken or turkey, potatoes roasted in the same pan, grilled tomatoes, and boiled scallions.

INGREDIENTS FOR FOUR

4 small, firm squash, preferably uniform in size

3 Tbsp (about) olive oil

½ tsp (about) dried leaf thyme

salt and pepper

To make: Split the squash lengthwise and, with a piece of waxed paper, brush the cut surfaces with olive oil. Sprinkle with thyme, salt, and pepper and cook under a hot broiler until done—about twenty minutes. It is not necessary to turn the squash.

PUFF PASTE

THE PREPARATION of puff paste has always been something of a bugaboo to cooks. There is no mystery to why this is so; making successful puff paste demands a high order of a special sort of technique. To expect even an experienced cook to prepare a perfect puff paste right off by following the classical recipe, and without a demonstration, is very like expecting a pianist, however able, to play one of the more difficult Chopin études at sight. And since most people know this, the most elegant of pastry doughs, only through disappointing encounters with the rather inanely named, and for the most part dull-tasting, "patty shells" and the commercially made "Napoleons" and turn-overs, it is easy to see why they forego attempting to make it. Actually, puff paste, the most flexible of doughs, is superb for *quiches*, open fruit pies (*tartes*), steak and kidney pie, chicken pie, beef Wellington, the much esteemed *tarte des demoiselles Tatin*, small hors d'oeuvre *barquettes* or *tartelettes*, and countless other dishes—many of them inexpensive, but none of them banal. In short, puff paste falls in that special category of elegant items of the French cuisine which exists only because of the skill of chefs. Anyone with the necessary money can buy *foie gras* and caviar, but even money can't buy the skill required to make good puff paste. To illustrate, a friend of mine asked me for the recipe for beef Wellington. He was going to be mar-ried in a fairly large town in one of the southern states and wanted to order this dish for the wedding recep-tion. I gave him the recipe, but warned that it could not be made with any crust other than puff paste. Some-time later he told me that he had inquired about the puff paste at the hotel where the reception was to be held and had been told that their cooks could not make it.

Simon Arbellot, one of the excellent writers for the French gastronomic magazine *Cuisine et Vins de France*, exemplified in one of his columns how puff paste is regarded by the experts: he characterized a restaurant he admired as "un maison de feuilleté et des truffes" (a puff paste and truffle establishment). While it is almost impossible to buy fresh truffles in the United States, we *can* make puff paste. It costs next to nothing except labor and time.

Mention of labor and time brings to mind one of the main reservations I have heard about making puff paste: "Oh, that's the dough you have to keep putting in the refrigerator and taking out again." Well, even though I am presenting a foolproof method of making puff paste, it nevertheless demands the same number of "resting and firming" periods in the refrigerator as the classical recipe. I would like to counter by asking, "What is so difficult about chilling dough for periods of fifteen minutes?" If you are properly organized— and if you mean to cook, you had better be—it is a simple matter to occupy yourself with other things that need doing while the dough is in the refrigerator. In any case, if you are not prepared to put up with the delays, don't bother making the dough.

The classical method for making puff paste consists of rolling out a rectangle of dough made with flour, water, and salt. A smaller rectangle of butter is placed on the dough rectangle. All four sides of the dough are then folded in over the butter to form a sort of package or envelope. This package is rolled out to form a large rectangle in which the butter is evenly distributed by pressing and rolling with the rolling pin. The rectangle is then folded in three as a letter is folded, the second fold covering the first fold. This folded package is rolled out again into a rectangle, but this time in the opposite direction—in other words, from the open sides of the package. This folding and rolling out is repeated six times, with a firming and resting period of fifteen minutes in the refrigerator after the second and fourth rolling. The French call these rollings *tours* (turns).

Puff paste ready for the oven consists of many very fine sheets of dough separated by an equal number of very fine sheets of butter. Since these layers produce the characteristic light flakiness of puff paste, the rolling and folding must be done as evenly as possible.

In other words, the real key to making puff paste is symmetry, a matter I shall go into later in this discussion.

All traditional instructions for making puff paste indicate that the dough and the butter should be of the same texture. It seems to me that this instruction has been a major preventive to the successful preparation of puff paste. The substances are so unlike each other that few people seem to know just what the statement means. Well, there is a very easy way of determining the correct balance of textures. If the dough, before the addition of the butter, holds together and, after twenty minutes in the refrigerator, rolls out easily, doesn't stick to the fingers, and doesn't pull, the texture is fine. Now take one-fourth pound of regular margarine (made with corn oil, but not the very soft sort) directly from the refrigerator. The texture of the margarine will be exactly the texture your butter should have. To arrive at this texture with chilled butter, you must work (*triturer*) and knead the chilled butter under cold water with your hands. (It will not do to allow it to thaw since, like everything else, butter thaws from the outside toward the center.) Since it is slippery, it is best to put the butter into a cloth which has been lightly sprinkled with flour. The object is to render the butter malleable, not soft. In other words, it should be kneaded to a state in which it can be rolled with the dough under firm, but not undue, pressure.

Before beginning the recipes I feel obliged to list a few of the things that can happen during the making of the dough. Please don't be put off by the number of warnings and the long list of rules. If I seem to overdo it, please attribute my excess to the number of times I have heard people say: "Why, I didn't know that" or "Why didn't the recipe say that?"

Warnings: If the dough is too rubbery—and I mean *before* the butter rectangle is placed on it—it will not maintain its shape when rolled. Puff paste cannot be made with such dough. Throw it away and start again.

If it is improperly worked and is too hard or lumpy, the butter very likely will break through the dough envelope. If the break is not a large one, sprinkle flour over it and continue rolling; by working carefully you can probably retrieve the situation.

If it is too soft, the butter will very likely break through the dough. In this case you will have an unretrievable mess—or at the very least, an uneven dough.

Rules: From the moment you first roll out the dough, place the butter on it, and enclose it as though in a package, you should make every effort to maintain strict symmetry in the thickness of the dough and the dimensions of each rolled-out rectangle. For example, if you roll out a rectangle eighteen inches long, it should be six inches wide. Obviously, if you fold the rectangle in three, as is required, and the ends that should meet flush are uneven, you will not have a proper distribution of the layers when the dough is rolled out again. Always roll and press in the same direction. In other words, turn the dough, not the rolling pin.

When cooking puff paste, it isn't necessary to butter the bottom or sides of the cooking utensil. On the contrary, if sugar is not mixed with the dough (sometimes it is), it is desirable to moisten the surface of the pan with water. Moisture causes the dough to adhere to the pan surface, which helps it to keep its shape.

Do not attempt to stretch puff paste after it has been

rolled out; the moment the heat hits it, the stretched part will return to its original shape. When rolling out dough for a pie or any other form, therefore, roll the dough larger than the size needed. Leftover dough can always be used for small tarts, hors d'oeuvre, or *fleurons* (see p. 236).

The most attractive glaze for puff paste is produced by lightly brushing the surface of the pastry with egg yolks mixed with a little water, milk, or cream. If, as with pastry shells, you want the dough to rise evenly on the cut edges, be careful that the glaze does not drip over them.

For certain pies and tarts it is best to cook the pastry shells before filling. A common (there are exceptions) instruction in this case is to prick the bottom of the dough with a fork and then cover it with uncooked rice or beans (to prevent the shell from puffing up too much, as it surely will if you do not take precautions). If you follow the instruction as sometimes given, however, you will have a fine time extracting the rice or beans from the dough into which they will have become embedded. Instead, prick the bottom of the dough with a fork, cut out a piece of waxed paper or foil slightly larger than the inside of the pan, butter the paper or foil well, place it in the shell buttered-side down, and pour the rice or beans on top of it, making sure that they do not touch the dough on the sides. When the dough on the sides of the shell is lightly browned, remove the paper with the rice or beans and allow the bottom crust to brown. The moment the shell is done, remove it from the pan and cool it on a grill. The rice or beans may be used over and over again.

The best rolling pin for any kind of pastry is the French type, which does not have handles, is the same thickness from end to end, and looks like a police baton (club).

When you have folded the butter in the dough and are ready to roll it into a rectangle, start off by pressing down with the rolling pin rather than rolling. Press down repeatedly and symmetrically from one end of the dough to the other. The object here is to distribute the butter evenly in the dough pocket. When you have a rough sort of rectangle, begin rolling, but do not roll over the ends, which could cause the pocket to break and release the butter. Instead, press down with the rolling pin, directing the butter away from the ends if too much has accumulated there.

When the dough is ready to be used—say, you want to make an uncovered pie (*tarte*)—roll the dough out to roughly the size of your pan plus a few inches extra on all sides. Place the pan over the dough and, after determining just which part of the dough will form the bottom (rather than the sides), roll that part thinner. The sides should be thicker than the bottom.

When you have fitted it in the pan, let the dough rest in the refrigerator for fifteen minutes before putting it in the oven. This helps the dough keep its shape.

When rolling puff paste dough, work methodically and smoothly. If you work too fast, you run the risk of toughening the dough; if you work too slowly, you run the risk of softening the butter too much.

Recipes for Puff Paste

The ratio of butter to flour determines the quality of puff paste, but it also determines the difficulty of handling it. Ideally the weight of the butter should equal the weight of the flour—a ratio difficult for beginners. My advice is to begin with an easy version.

Note: Butter is definitely preferable to margarine; nevertheless, margarine makes excellent puff paste. But don't forget that margarine melts very rapidly. If necessary, chill it longer than directed. In fact, when using margarine, it is a good idea to chill all the ingredients, including the flour.

Before attempting any of the following recipes, please read the warnings and rules above.

FOOLPROOF PUFF PASTE

Although the method employed in this recipe is radically different from the classical one, it produces a very good puff paste indeed. In any case, it is an ideal recipe to learn from, as attempting it will result in satisfaction rather than frustration and rejection of the whole idea. Too, once your hand is in, you may try some of the other recipes.

INGREDIENTS FOR TWO EIGHT-INCH CRUSTS

½ lb butter, chilled

2 cups all-purpose flour

1 tsp salt

slightly less than ½ cup water, chilled

To make: In a bowl mix the flour, one-half the butter (one-fourth pound), the salt, and the water to make a firm, but flexible, dough. Cut the butter into the flour with a knife and add the water a little at a time. Use only as much water as needed; but if you need more than one-half cup, don't hesitate to add a little. When the dough is well mixed but not yet cohesive, dump it

The first step in making foolproof puff paste. Part of the butter is cut into the flour and salt with two knives.

Water has been added to the flour, butter, and salt mixture, and the whole has been amalgamated.

The dough, which has been "resting" in the refrigerator, is flanked by the chopped butter and the extra flour which will be needed in handling it.

The rolled-out dough with one-third of the remaining butter chopped and disposed on the dough.

The dough properly folded. It will now be chilled for fifteen minutes and then rolled out again lengthwise, away from the folds visible. Chopped butter will again be disposed as in the previous photograph, and the dough will again be folded and chilled. As the recipe indicates, this is done three times in all.

The dough rolled out after the first folding-in of the butter. Bits of the butter enfolded in the dough are visible.

A quiche Lorraine *(top) made with the foolproof puff paste dough (see p. 77 for the recipe).*

An apple tart (bottom) made with the foolproof puff paste dough (see p. 240 for the recipe).

out onto the pastry board and work it with your hands until it is a smooth mass and does not stick to the fingers. Form a ball of the dough, wrap it well in waxed paper, and chill it in the refrigerator (not in the freezer) for twenty minutes. Then roll out the dough into a large rectangle, somewhat under one-fourth-inch thick. Cut the remaining one-fourth pound of firmly chilled, but not hard, butter into three pieces. Cut one of the three pieces into small, less-than-pea-sized pieces. Put the other two uncut pieces in the refrigerator. Dispose the small pieces of butter evenly over the entire surface of the dough rectangle. Fold the rectangle as a business letter is folded—that is in three, the second fold covering the first fold. Then fold in three in the opposite direction to the first folding. Wrap again and chill in the refrigerator for fifteen minutes. Repeat the sequence—rolling out the dough into a large rectangle, placing cut-up butter on it, folding it in three in two directions successively, and chilling it—two more times, or three times in all. The dough is then ready to be used.

CLASSICAL PUFF PASTE

INGREDIENTS FOR FIVE EIGHT-INCH CRUSTS

5 cups all-purpose flour

17 ounces butter

1 tsp salt

1 cup, or a little more, water (It is difficult to be exact, since flavors vary in absorption quality.)

To make: Put the flour and salt in a bowl and mix lightly. Add water, a tablespoon at a time, mixing lightly with a fork. When the dough begins to hold together somewhat, work with a knife and fork, cutting and stirring to make as homogeneous a mass as possible. Then dump the dough out onto a pastry marble or board. With your hands, working the dough as little as possible, form the dough into a cohesive mass. In other words, it should be fairly smooth and hold together. If it does not, add a little water or, if you have the time, cover the dough with a bowl and let the moisture permeate the mixture for fifteen minutes (not in the refrigerator). Then roll the dough into a ball, wrap it in waxed paper, and chill it in the refrigerator (not in the freezer or directly on ice) for twenty minutes. Just before the twenty minutes are up, prepare the butter as described in the introductory remarks above (see p. 223). Roll out the dough into a rectangle, about twelve inches long by eight inches wide. Mold the butter into a smaller rectangle and place it on the dough. Fold the two ends of the dough in, then the two sides, to form a package, pressing down with a rolling pin to seal the seams. Wrap the package in waxed paper and let it rest for ten minutes in the refrigerator. Then commence proceedings by pressing down with the rolling pin and then rolling to make a rectangle about eighteen inches long and six inches wide, keeping the dough of even thickness throughout. Now fold the rectangle in three as a business letter is folded, the second fold covering the first fold. Roll out again into a rectangle, but this time in the opposite direction, working from the open sides of the folded rectangle. When the rectangle is again eighteen inches long and six inches wide, fold it in three, wrap it, and put it in the refrigerator for fifteen minutes. Repeat the same sequence as above two more times. That is, roll out four more rectangles, chilling the dough for fifteen minutes between the fourth and sixth turns, changing the direction of the rolling each time. The dough is then ready to use, but, of course, it must be rolled to the thickness required for your purpose, which can range from less than one-eighth inch to considerably thicker dough. Since few people have pastry marbles or boards large enough to handle a large quantity of dough, it is a simple matter to halve the quantity of this recipe.

Note: Although it is nice to have a professional pastry marble or a good-sized pastry board, Americans are good at improvising and I am sure you won't be put off by the lack of a standard rolling surface. I recall seeing a photograph of a French chef demonstrating the making of puff paste to a queen mother (I have forgotten of which country). The caption under the photograph indicated that the chef had told her that it was absolutely essential to have a chilled pastry marble in order to make puff paste. One way of getting around that is simply to use a thoroughly chilled quart bottle of beer as a rolling pin. It works fine.

CLASSICAL PUFF PASTE WITH EGG

This puff paste is known as Viennese. The addition of egg yolks makes for easier handling and a crust that maintains its crispness.

INGREDIENTS FOR THREE EIGHT-INCH CRUSTS

3 cups all-purpose flour

10 ounces butter

2 egg yolks, lightly beaten

juice of ½ lemon

⅓ cup water

¼ tsp salt

[233]

To make: Mix one cup of the flour with all of the butter, cutting it in with a knife and then working it with your hands until smooth. Make a dough of the remaining two cups of flour, the egg yolks, lemon juice, salt, and water. Roll the dough out into a large rectangle. Form the butter-flour mixture into a much smaller rectangle and place it on the dough rectangle. Fold the two sides of the dough over the butter-flour rectangle, leaving the ends open, and with a rolling pin, pressing and rolling, roll out a large rectangle. Do not allow the butter to squeeze out on the ends. Fold in three as a business letter is folded, the second fold covering the first; then roll out again, but in the other direction, with the open sides of the folds toward you. Repeat this sequence five times (six turns in all), chilling the dough for fifteen minutes after the second and fourth turn.

INSTANT PUFF PASTE

This is an easy, quick, and quite effective way of making a crust that is not exactly puff paste, but is close enough to make it worthwhile. It is perfect, for example, as a top crust for a casserole of beef stew, creamed chicken, or fish in a cream sauce.

INGREDIENTS FOR FOUR EIGHT-INCH CRUSTS

4 cups all-purpose flour

1 lb and 3 tsp butter

¼ tsp salt

1¾ cups water

To make: In a bowl mix the flour and the salt, and cut in the butter with a knife or two knives. Then add the water, little by little, until the dough begins to hold together. Dump the contents of the bowl onto a pastry board and mix it well with your hands. Roll it into a ball, wrap in waxed paper, and chill in the refrigerator for twenty minutes. Then, working quickly but smoothly, roll the dough out into a large rectangle, fold it in three, and, in the opposite direction from the initial rolling, with the sides of the package toward you, roll it out again. Do this four times, one after the other, turning the dough in the opposite direction each time, and the dough is ready to be used. If your kitchen is quite warm, chill the dough after the second rolling and chill it again after completion and before baking.

Some Puff Paste Recipes

It would require another good-sized book to adequately cover the traditional uses of puff paste—a task I am not undertaking here—but I would like to indicate a few less traditional ways of using it. I encountered a good example of the flexibility of puff paste one day in Paris at lunch at Weber on the rue Royale. (This excellent restaurant closed its doors only a few years after Larue at the other end of the block gave up the ghost to be replaced by an establishment named Queenie's. These changes were hardly for the better, but the restaurant business is not noted for sentiment, and the shades of Boni de Castellane, Marcel Proust, the Russian grand dukes, Alphonse Daudet, and countless other illustrious habitués could not pay the bills.) In any case—to get back to Weber and that lunch—I ordered what the menu listed as chicken pie. It turned out to be a beautiful sauté of chicken with a delicious sauce, but the only token to the American concept of pie was a large, attractively shaped piece of very crisp puff paste, which, well heated, had been placed on top. While technically the dish was not a pie, it was excellent eating and, of course, there was no question of soggy pie crust. It occurred to me that the large piece of crust was an enlarged version of the traditional French *fleuron*—a shaped piece of puff paste (cut with a form into hearts, stars, and crescents) which is browned and glazed in the oven and served as an attractive garnish to many sauced dishes.

FLEURONS

Fleurons are small pieces of puff paste generally cut out with special forms, the commonest of which is the crescent. Glazed and browned in the oven, they make an attractive and appetizing garnish to sauced dishes, especially those with light-colored sauces, such as *filet de sole Normande* or chicken fricassee. They are an ideal way of using up leftover bits of puff paste which, placed side by side slightly overlapping, can be rolled into a sheet of dough. If you don't have the regular forms, use cookie cutters (if they are not too large) or merely press out rounds and bake them as they are or cut them in half before baking. A few very small *fleurons* sprinkled on the surface of creamed soups look attractive and add a bit of texture. As a variation, roll out the dough very thin, sprinkle half of it with a little paprika and very finely grated cheddar cheese, fold over the other half, roll out again, and cut up as you wish.

[236]

TARTE AUX POMMES

The ingredients for this apple tart are simplicity itself, but the result is one of the glories of French cuisine. A friend of mine described it as quite the opposite of most pies, because he enjoys the crust even more than the filling. It is not a heavy dessert.

4 golden delicious or 5 Macintosh apples, peeled, cored, and roughly chopped

6 golden delicious or 7 Macintosh apples, peeled, quartered, cored, and sliced into crescents ⅛ inch thick

puff paste

3 ounces butter

2 cups granulated white sugar

juice of ½ lemon

1 egg yolk

2 Tbsp cream, milk, or water

4 Tbsp apricot jelly, jam, or preserves

To make: Put a few tablespoons of water into a heavy-bottomed pot. Add the chopped apples and one-half cup of sugar, and cook until quite soft. If they seem very watery, cook the apples until most of the liquid has evaporated. Mash thoroughly while hot, and set aside to cool. Mix the remaining apples with one cup of sugar and the lemon juice. Stir and toss well. Set

[2 3 7]

aside for thirty minutes to allow the apples to render some of their moisture. Roll out the dough, taking care to roll very thin the part that will form the under-crust. The sides should be somewhat thicker and not skimpy. Spread the cooled mashed apples over the bottom of the tart. Then, starting from dead center, lay concentric overlapping rings of the drained apple crescents over the apple puree. To the extent that you do this symmetrically, the finished tart will be attractive in appearance. Preheat the oven to 450°. Cut the butter into pea-sized pieces and distribute them evenly on the slices. With a fork, press the sides of the dough to make a uniform serrated pattern. Mix the egg yolk and cream and brush the parts of the dough not covered by the apples with the mixture. Put the tart into a 450° oven and cook until the sides are lightly browned. Then turn the heat down to 400°. After the tart is in the oven, put the drained apple juice, one-half cup of sugar, and the apricot jelly into a pot and cook until it is thick, but not carmelized. Pour this syrup evenly over the tart when you turn down the heat to 400°. Brush some over the crust also. The pie is done when the crust at the sides is a mahogany brown.

To serve: This tart is best served warm, and it reheats very well. If you want something more than a light dessert, top the warm tart with chilled whipped cream.

The French like to undersweeten tarts such as this and add sugar from a shaker at the table; this makes sense, since, as with salt, some people like more sugar than others.

Note: I have seen recipes that direct one to partially cook the pastry shell before adding the apples. There is nothing wrong with this procedure if the dough is thick. The thickness of the crust I have in mind is not much more than one-sixteenth of an inch.

A SUBSTITUTE FOR PATTY SHELLS

I don't like the standard puff paste shells; their very construction assures that the inner part of the shell will be tough. Instead of rejecting them and letting it go at that, however, I have devised a method that produces the same useful sizes of patty shells with complete crispness throughout. One of the agreeable aspects of the standard patty shell (what a term!) is that they don't require forms. My method does, but adequate forms can be made very easily; use a triple thickness of heavy aluminum foil to make whatever shape or size you wish by pressing and molding the foil over a bowl, saucer, dish, or whatever. This way you can make pastry shells of every size, but the sizes that interest me most are ones not generally available in metal, pyrex, or earthenware—sizes to hold a single portion of a luncheon entrée and a single portion of a dinner entrée. These improvised shells are attractive and, more important, they facilitate serving since they and their filling can be kept warm and assembled just before serving. They can also be used for desserts—peach tart with *crème pâtissière*, for example. A number of the better Parisian restaurants serve desserts of this sort and, as a matter of course, assemble them just before serving.

A famous three-star restaurant in Paris has as a specialty *crevettes* (small shrimp) with a sauce served in a box made by hollowing out a section of a small loaf of square, white bread, removing the crusts, and deep-frying it or brushing it with butter and browning in the oven. As an idea it is all right—traditional, in fact—but the damned box is too hard to cut with ease, and there is always the danger that it will slide into your lap. The same mixture served in a puff paste crust would far transcend the gimmicky box, both in delicacy and practicality.

Another way to use the improvised forms is for individual steak and kidney pies, chicken pies, or just plain beef pies. You will notice that your guests eat every crumb.

In making these pastry shells, the only warning I give is that the sides of the form should be gently sloping. Puff paste gets very soft when the heat hits it and before it crisps; a shell with vertical sides will collapse on you —I mean, in the pan.

STRASBOURG APPLE TART

In Alsace (the French province bordering on Germany of which Strasbourg is the most important city) apples are an important part of the diet—not only for desserts but as a garnish for pork in the form of applesauce as an ingredient to mix with red cabbage and sauerkraut. The most typical desserts of the region are fruit pies: apple, plum, and particularly mirabelle (a small yellow plum the size of a large olive, which does not grow in America).

Strasbourg apple tart differs from the more sophisticated *tarte des demoiselles Tatin* (see p. 246) in that the apple slices need not be arranged so elaborately and that a mixture of egg yolks, cream, sugar, and vanilla is added. The tart is baked only until the custard is set and slightly brown on top.

INGREDIENTS FOR AN EIGHT AND ONE-HALF–INCH PIE

enough puff paste to fit an 8½-inch pie pan with sides to spare (Roll out the dough that will form the bottom crust very thin. Leave the part that will form the sides quite thick; they will puff up nicely and be crisp.)

4 large golden delicious apples, peeled, cored, and sliced into segments the size of orange sections

5 egg yolks

1 Tbsp milk

½ cup heavy cream

1 tsp vanilla

¾ cup granulated sugar

½ cup confectioners sugar

2 Tbsp butter, chopped

To make: Preheat the oven to 400°. Roll out the dough as indicated above. Fit it into the pan without pulling or stretching. Add the apples, fitting them in neatly. Sprinkle the apples with the granulated sugar and chopped butter. Mix one egg yolk with the milk and brush the edges of the pie dough with the mixture. Bake the pie in a 400° oven until the apples are just soft (approximately fifty minutes). If during the cooking the crust seems to be browning too fast, lower the heat first to 350°, then, if necessary, to 300°. Mix, but do not beat, the cream, vanilla, remaining egg yolks, and confectioners sugar, and pour over the apples. (If you did not use all of the egg yolk mixed with milk, add it to the custard.) Continue baking until the custard is just set and the surface is nicely browned.

To serve: This tart may be served hot, tepid, or cold. I prefer it tepid.

STRAWBERRY TART WITH PUFF PASTE CRUST

Strawberry tart with puff paste crust is a strawberry-season standby in good French restaurants.

INGREDIENTS

puff paste for a 12 x 5 inch tart

1 egg yolk

2 Tbsp milk or cream

2 quarts strawberries

1 cup sugar or to taste

juice of ½ lemon

To make: The crust—usually an elongated rectangle with built-up edges—is cooked in advance and allowed to cool on a rack. Before adding the side strips (which should be three-fourths inch wide) to the bottom dough, brush the edges of the rectangle with water to assure that the strips will adhere. Then place the strips as symmetrically as possible and brush them with a mixture of egg yolk and milk or egg yolk and cream, but be careful not to dribble the mixture over the sides of the strips or they won't puff up. The bottom part of the rectangle—the part within the strips which will hold the strawberries—must be perforated thoroughly with a fork to prevent the puff paste from puffing up too much. The sides, on the contrary, should be allowed to puff up as much as they can. Cook the shell or crust in a preheated 450° oven; it isn't necessary to butter the baking pan.

While the puff paste shell is baking, clean the strawberries. Wash and dry them quickly, put them in a bowl and add sugar to taste along with the juice of one-half a lemon for one quart of strawberries. Put the berries in the refrigerator. Thirty minutes before serving the tart, drain the berries and put them back into the refrigerator, but don't throw away the juice. Put it in a small pot and reduce it over low heat until it thickens, but not into candy; it must be just thick enough when it has cooled to pour over the berries.

To prepare for serving, fit the berries, stem side down, into the pastry shell. Arrange them as symmetrically as possible. Then very carefully pour the reduced juice over the berries. There should only be enough to lightly cover each strawberry.

To serve: Serve immediately and pass a sugar shaker for those who like their desserts very sweet.

Note: In Chicago I was once served a strawberry tart that was glazed, so help me God, with Jello. For sheer banality, that was it.

STEAK AND KIDNEY PIE

Steak and kidney pie is one of the masterpieces of English cuisine. With its succulent gravy, faint flavor of game imparted by the kidneys and mushrooms, two meat textures, and delicate puff paste crust—it is an almost perfect entrée. Steak and kidney pie doesn't need a garnish; it is easy to serve; and it is never banal. There are those who make a to-do about using veal rather than beef kidneys, which they claim are traditional. Without going into the validity of their claim—in fact, I'll concede it—I still opt for the better-tasting, finer-textured veal kidneys.

INGREDIENTS FOR FOUR

2 lb lean round steak cut into strips, 1½ inches long but 1½ inches thick

6 shallots or 1 bunch of scallions, finely chopped (If you use scallions, reject only the top half of the green parts.)

1 veal kidney, sliced into pieces the size of a hazelnut (Reject all nerves and membranes.)

1½ ounces dried mushrooms, preferably Polish, or 4 ounces fresh mushrooms

small piece bay leaf, the size of a dime

pinch of dried leaf thyme (⅛ tsp)

salt and pepper

1 Tbsp parsley, very finely chopped

2 Tbsp flour

beef or chicken stock, to cover

2 to 3 Tbsp butter or oil

½ cup fine dry Madeira wine

puff paste

egg yolk (optional)

2 Tbsp cream, milk, or water (optional)

To make: If you use dried mushrooms, wash them quickly in a colander with cold water. Put them in a small pot with water to cover and cook for fifteen minutes over low heat. Allow them to cool, chop roughly, and return to their liquid, which is not thrown away—it is the veritable essence of mushrooms. If you use fresh mushrooms, wipe them (do not wash unless they are exceptionally dirty, and then as quickly as possible). Do not peel, but trim off the tough ends of the stems. Slice them and sauté in butter or oil for five minutes over very low heat.

Heat the butter or oil in a skillet, add the round steak and kidneys, and over high heat brown the pieces on all sides. When this is done, turn the heat down to very low, push the pieces of meat to one side, and add the shallots or scallions. Sauté until quite soft, stirring frequently. If the pan becomes dry at any point, add more butter or oil. When the shallots or scallions are soft, add the bay leaf, thyme, parsley, and salt and pepper, and cook for one minute more, stirring constantly. Now turn the heat up to very high, dust the flour over the contents of the pan, and, stirring very swiftly, brown the flour. When the flour is lightly browned, add the mushrooms with their liquid and enough stock to cover the meat. Bring to a boil, stirring constantly to blend the flour into the stock; then turn down the heat to very low. Cook until the beef is tender —about one hour and thirty minutes. As the liquid reduces, add the Madeira wine. Stir frequently. Set aside to cool.

Roll out the puff paste very thin—about one-eighth inch thick. Fit a section of it in a relatively shallow (approximately three and one-half inches high), rectangular, ovenproof glass baking dish. Allow at least one and one-half inches over the edges. Fill with the meat mixture, but no higher than one-eighth inch from the top. Cover with a sheet of puff paste one inch larger than the dimensions of the dish. With your hands arrange the edges of the bottom and top crust as evenly as possible and press them firmly on the rim of the dish.

Make a fluted pattern all around with a fork, pressing down firmly. Make two holes the circumference of a cigarette in the top of the crust and insert into each a rolled piece of stiff paper about two inches long. These chimneys allow the gravy to bubble up without breaking the crust.

Preheat the oven to 400°. If you are so inclined, decorate the top crust. Ideally, forms or dies in various shapes are used to cut out pieces of the leftover puff paste dough. Failing these, you can do wonders with strips cut with a knife and wound around the chimneys; you can even make elaborate designs, if you are deft enough. Before adding the decorative pieces of dough, brush the entire top surface of the pie with a mixture of egg yolk and a little cream, milk, or water. The decorations will adhere to this. Then brush the tops of the decorations with the same mixture. Cook the pie in a 400° oven until the crust is nicely browned and the gravy is bubbling in the chimneys.

Note: If you make steak and kidney pie once, I assure you that you will make it again. Of course, the recipe serves as a prototype for all sorts of pies—chicken, beef, beef with oysters, turkey, and even fish.

TARTE DES DEMOISELLES TATIN

Another version of the always popular apple tart, the *tarte des demoiselles Tatin* is unique; its crust is superimposed on a layer of apples which, in turn, are placed on a layer of butter and another layer of confectioners sugar. Perhaps you recognize the familiar upside-down principle, but with puff paste the result is a very crisp crust (never soggy) and nicely carmelized apples.

INGREDIENTS FOR FIVE OR SIX

puff paste

4 golden delicious apples, peeled, cored, and sliced into segments

3 Tbsp butter, or more (enough to butter the pan heavily)

3 Tbsp butter, chopped (to put on top of the apples)

1 egg yolk

1 Tbsp milk

confectioners sugar (enough to make a layer ⅓ inch thick)

To make: Preheat the oven to 450°. Butter a pan or dish. (An eight-and-one-half-inch pie tin will do if it is at least two inches deep, but a deeper, fireproof glass or glazed earthenware dish is far better. It need not be round; merely shape your dough to accommodate the form.) Add the confectioners sugar, apples, and then the chopped butter. Roll out the dough so that it is about two inches wider than the dish or tin on all sides. Fit this evenly over the apples; then press the edges down the sides of the pan so that the apples are completely covered. Mix the egg yolk and milk and brush the surface of the dough with the mixture. Slash the dough in five places to allow the steam to escape. Bake the tart in a 450° oven until the dough becomes nicely browned. After twenty minutes of baking, tilt the dish in order to see if the sauce is becoming carmelized. If it is browning too rapidly, cover the dough with aluminum foil and continue cooking until the apples are carmelized.

If the apples were too watery or the oven registration was incorrect, the dough may be thoroughly cooked but the apples not carmelized. If so, take the tart from the oven and, just before serving it, place a large oven-proof plate over the baking dish to catch the tart and, with a quick turn, deposit it on the plate. The crust will now be on the bottom. Sprinkle the apples lightly with confectioners sugar and glaze them under a medium broiler flame; be sure that they are not too close to the flame. In any case, watch the tart carefully; confectioners sugar burns very quickly.

To serve: Serve hot or tepid with unsweetened whipped cream.

Note: This tart can be made in advance and reheated. If you intend to reheat it, leave the tart in its baking dish until just before serving, reheat, and turn onto a plate.

MEAT LOAF IN A PUFF PASTE CRUST

I devised this recipe for meat loaf as a sort of riposte to beef Wellington. I like beef Wellington, but the retail price of beef fillet irritates me. Besides, fillet of beef from our usually overfattened American cattle is not the most savory cut of beef, although it has everything else in its favor: it has no bones, is an ideal shape and size for rapid cooking, and can be served quite rare. This meat loaf, which is made with ground round steak and vegetables, can be shaped to resemble beef fillet. It doesn't take long to cook, is juicy, and can also be served somewhat rare. It tastes equally good hot, tepid, or cold and is splendid as part of a buffet.

INGREDIENTS FOR FOUR TO SIX

2 lb ground round steak (I suggest a minimum of one pound of meat for three people, and then only if you are serving it as a buffet dish along with other appetizing items. In my experience, when served as an entrée, people taste it and just keep on eating; on one occasion, three of us just about finished one loaf made from over two pounds of meat.)

3 Tbsp butter or oil

2 bunches scallions (with half the green parts), chopped

2 medium carrots, very finely grated

1 stalk celery (with its leaves), very, very finely chopped

2 Tbsp parsley, finely chopped

1 tsp dried basil

salt and pepper

½ cup dry white bread crumbs

beef bouillon

2 egg yolks, lightly beaten

1 egg yolk

cream, milk, or water

FOR THE SAUCE

2 to 3 cups beef bouillon

3 Tbsp tomato paste

½ tsp dried basil

2 Tbsp dry Madeira wine (optional)

To make: Heat the butter or oil in a heavy-bottomed skillet. Add the scallions, carrots, celery, parsley, one teaspoon basil, salt, and pepper. Cook covered over very low heat until the mixture is soft and blends easily. Set aside to cool.

Soak the bread crumbs with just enough beef bouillon to moisten them thoroughly. Add to the cooked vegetable mixture.

In a large bowl, mix the ground meat with the vegetables and crumb mixture. When partially mixed, add the two lightly beaten egg yolks and continue mixing until well blended. It is possible to do the mixing entirely with a large spoon or fork, but I use my hands, which really do the job.

Preheat the oven to 350°. In a shallow roasting pan or on a doubled piece of heavy aluminum foil, shape the meat into a long loaf. Take care that the roll does not have obvious cracks, as these will enlarge during the cooking and make the roll difficult to handle later on when you are putting it in the pastry crust. Put the loaf in a 350° oven and cook from forty-five minutes to one hour. After forty-five minutes the meat will have rendered its fat and still be somewhat rare in the center. If you like meat loaf well done, cook for one hour; in any case, it will cook a little more during the cooking of the pastry crust. Remove the meat loaf from the cooking pan and set it aside for thirty minutes to cool. Reject the fat in the pan.

Roll out the puff paste into a rectangle somewhat larger than you will need to cover the meat loaf. I like the crust very thin (one-eighth inch), but just under one-fourth inch will do. Since the center of the rectangle of dough will form the top of the meat loaf, it is advisable to roll the outer parts which will form the bottom crust thinner than the other part. If the dough is too thick on the bottom, given the weight of the meat, it will be tough when cooked.

Preheat the oven to 450°. When the rectangle of dough is rolled out, place the cooled meat loaf on it, top-side down. Fold one side over the roll, note how far it goes beyond the center where it will meet the other side, and trim off what will not be needed. Do the same on the other side. The two sides should (without pulling or stretching the dough) overlap by a mere one-half inch. Brush the edge of one side with a mixture of one egg yolk and cream, milk, or water, cover with the other side, and press down firmly with your hand. Make neat folds of the ends, press them together, and trim off excess dough. Turn the meat loaf over and place it on a pastry sheet or heavy foil which has been lightly brushed with water. Now brush the top and sides with the egg yolk mixture, taking care that it does not run off into the pan. Decorate with shapes made of the leftover dough. These shapes are best made with forms expressly for this purpose (which can be purchased from shops that sell French cooking utensils), but with a little patience you can cut them out with a sharp knife. Brush the surface, but not the sides, of the decorations with the egg yolk mixture.

Put the meat loaf in a 450° oven, toward the top of the oven rather than the bottom, and cook until the pastry is nicely browned—about thirty to forty-five minutes.

To serve: Serve with a sauce made by simmering the beef stock, tomato paste, and one-half teaspoon dried basil for thirty minutes. If you have some good dry Madeira wine at hand, add two tablespoons to the sauce.

DESSERTS

I HAVE observed that the American, male or female, who is at all knowledgeable about food and wines, will rebel at the idea of a dessert without intrinsic culinary interest that is oversweet and overfilling—mince pie, for example. The same American will respond favorably to a dessert that is carefully designed to add an elegantly sweet fillip to a meal but does not overwhelm or one that is enough of a culinary achievement to render the factor of calories irrelevant. This makes sense to me; perdition is much less difficult to accept if the sin is worth it.

At the top of the list of light, but elegant, desserts I place those with a fruit base—compotes, sherbets, soufflés, and certain combination desserts. At the bottom of the list I nominate the disaster known as *Mont Blanc*, a sweet puree of chestnuts smothered with whipped cream. (Actually, *Mont Blanc* is a good dessert, but not something one would want after a heavy meal. It could be served after consommé, a veal scallop, and plain lettuce salad.)

FRESH PEARS
WITH COMPOTE OF STRAWBERRIES

To decide just what dessert to serve at the end of a large meal is often a problem: it shouldn't be too heavy, but it should have character; it shouldn't be too sweet, but it should satisfactorily provide a cadence to the meal. I like fresh pears with compote of strawberries, a dessert which, although easy to make, must be assembled no more than a few minutes before it is to be served.

INGREDIENTS FOR SIX

3 large, dead-ripe but unblemished Comice pears, well chilled

1 quart strawberries, prepared as on p. 254

eau de vie de framboise (This Alsatian liqueur is expensive, but a little goes a long way. Served in inhalator glasses with black coffee, nothing can compare with it.)

To make: The strawberries should be prepared in advance and chilled in the refrigerator. A few minutes

before serving, peel the pears, halve them, and carefully remove the core part of each half. Put one-half
a pear on each plate, garnish each with one-sixth of
the strawberries and two tablespoons of the compote
juice. Then, over each pear half pour one jigger, or a
little more, of the *eau de vie de framboise.*

To serve: Serve with a few first-quality cookies on the
side.

Note: A nice variation is to sprinkle finely crushed almond macaroons over the pear halves before adding
the strawberries and the *eau de vie.* (Dry four or five
macaroons in a slow oven, allow them to cool, and
pulverize them with a rolling pin.)

COMPOTE OF STRAWBERRIES

If compote of strawberries strikes you as an attempt
at gilding the lily, please reserve criticism until you
have tasted the result. I would be the first to agree that
a freshly picked strawberry needs no embellishment
beyond a sprinkle of sugar, but (unless you grow your
own) we must deal with a strawberry that has spent a
certain amount of time in travel and storage. No blame
is involved here; that's simply the way things are. We
shouldn't forget that, unlike the "good old days" when
one ate strawberries only in season, we now have them
almost all year round.

In any case, whether your strawberries are tired or
not, the following recipe enhances their flavor without
affecting their texture. In fact, most people upon first
tasting this compote assume that the strawberries have
been marinated in something too subtle to identify.

INGREDIENTS FOR SIX

2 quarts strawberries

*1 to 1½ cups sugar (depending on the sweetness
of the berries)*

⅕ cup water

juice of 1 medium lemon

To make: Hull the berries, but do not wash them. Cook
the sugar, water, and lemon juice until the sugar is
completely dissolved, stirring from time to time. When
the syrup is smooth and boiling, rapidly wash the
hulled berries in a colander, drain well, and throw
them into the syrup. Remove the pot from the heat
and very quickly toss and mix the berries in the syrup
with the object of distributing the heat of the syrup
uniformly throughout the strawberries. If your pot is
large enough and you have a light hand, this can be
done without bruising the berries. When the berries
have cooled, put them in the refrigerator until needed.

To serve: The compote can be served in any of the
following manners.

Garnish the strawberries with whipped cream and
serve cookies on the side.

On each plate place three or four ladyfingers, cover
with strawberries, and garnish with whipped cream.

On each serving of berries sprinkle one tablespoon of
crushed, dried almond macaroons which have imbibed
a good sprinkling of sherry or Marsala wine. Garnish
with whipped cream.

Serve in the traditional fashion, *Eaton Mess*: crush
the berries and mix into sweetened whipped cream.

Strawberries cooked in this fashion are good served with other fruits, cooked or uncooked (see p. 253).

SALAD OF ORANGES, BANANAS, AND APPLE
WITH GRAND MARNIER

Salad of oranges, bananas, and apple, a seemingly ordinary combination, results in more than its parts might suggest. It is refreshing and light—just right for the culmination of a fairly rich meal. Its only inconvenience is that it must be assembled only moments before it is served. The oranges and the lemon (which is used to point up the flavor of the fruits) may be sliced in advance, covered with clear plastic wrap, and chilled, but the bananas and apple should be added just before serving.

INGREDIENTS FOR SIX TO EIGHT

5 large, first-quality navel oranges

3 firm bananas

1 golden delicious apple, peeled and cubed

juice of 1 small lemon

sugar, to taste

½ cup Grand Marnier liqueur

To make: Peel the oranges, making sure to remove all the white pulp next to the skin. With a sharp knife, slice them—not in full, but in quarter, slices and as thin as you can manage. Through a strainer, squeeze the lemon juice on the orange slices. Just before serving, peel and slice the bananas, which, by the way, are better if you quarter them lengthwise and then slice them. Quarter, peel, and cube the apple and incorporate it into the mixture. Add as much sugar as suits you and mix thoroughly. Add the Grand Marnier, and that's all there is to it. I can assure you the salad won't be received without appreciation. (Incidentally, this recipe has nothing to do with that disaster called fruit cup, very often made with canned fruit, which some choose to serve as an appetizer.)

CRUSHED ALMOND MACAROONS
WITH ICE CREAM

Crushed almond macaroons with ice cream is delicious if you can find first-quality almond macaroons; the coconut variety simply won't do. Unlike most, this ice cream garnish is not oversweet, and it provides a contrasting texture that sets off the creaminess of good ice cream. It is not as harsh as chopped nuts and not as indeterminate as the customary slippery garnishes of bananas and fruit syrups. This dessert is a crispy and creamy combination which, I would go so far as to say, pleases just about everyone.

INGREDIENTS FOR FOUR

1 pint best-quality vanilla ice cream

5 almond macaroons

To make: Dry the macaroons in a 200° oven until crisp but not browned. Let them cool. With a rolling pin crush them until they resemble a fine meal.

To serve: Put the ice cream on the plates and completely coat each serving with the crushed macaroons. It's as simple as that, but I believe you will be surprised at the enthusiasm this dessert will spark.

[2 5 7]

CHOCOLATE SPONGECAKE

Chocolate spongecake (the French classic *le Marquis*) is ordinarily made in round pans, but for the purpose of this recipe I prefer a square ten-inch pan at least two inches high. I have served this cake often, and the whipped cream and shaved chocolate are definitely preferred to icing by most people. The cake can be presented attractively cut into slices with a large bowl of cream profusely sprinkled with chocolate shavings on the side.

INGREDIENTS FOR TEN TO TWELVE

5 ounces semisweet chocolate

2 ounces unsweetened chocolate

3 Tbsp hot, strong coffee

¼ lb butter

6 egg yolks

1¼ cups and 2 Tbsp granulated sugar

7 egg whites

⅛ tsp salt

1¼ cups all-purpose flour

FOR THE WHIPPED CREAM

1½ pints heavy cream

2 Tbsp granulated sugar

1 bar semisweet or unsweetened chocolate, refrigerated

To make: Preheat oven to 350°. In a double boiler melt the semisweet chocolate and the unsweetened chocolate. Add the hot coffee and salt and, when the chocolate has thoroughly melted, remove the top section of the double boiler from the water and set aside. Cut the butter into pieces and add to the melted chocolate. Separate seven eggs, being careful not to allow so much as a speck of yolk to fall into the whites, which should be put into a freshly washed and dried bowl. Put the yolks in a very large bowl, in which the cake mixture will be assembled. (You will, of course, end up with an unused yolk. If you wish, put it in a small bowl, cover with water, and put in the refrigerator. Use it the next day in an omelet or in scrambled eggs.) Add one and one-fourth cups sugar to the yolks and with a beater—electric or hand—mix until the yolks and sugar are perfectly amalgamated, at which time the mixture should be a light-lemon color. It is better to overdo the beating than underdo. Add the melted chocolate and butter to the yolks and sugar and beat until thoroughly mixed. Next add two tablespoons granulated sugar to the egg whites and beat—with a wire whisk, if you have one, or with an electric or hand beater. Be sure the beater is clean. The whites should be stiff enough to form a peak when the beater is lifted out, but they should not be dry. The next step is crucial, but not really risky. Measure out the flour and put it beside the large bowl containing the yolk-chocolate mixture. With a rubber spatula scoop out about one fifth of the egg whites into the yolk-chocolate mixture, dust with about one-fifth of the flour, and mix thoroughly. Next, add the other four-fifths of the egg whites and the flour and mix, but lightly. The best way is to blend with the rubber spatula with a sweeping motion—down to the bottom on one side, across the bottom, then up and over. To the extent that all the ingredients are amalgamated and blended with a light hand, the cake will be light. And don't worry if there are a few bits of egg white visible; it is better to have them than a subdued mixture. Pour the mixture into a pan which you have lined, on the bottom only, with waxed paper, but butter the bottom of the pan before putting down the paper and butter the paper after you have placed it in the pan. Cook the cake for forty-five minutes, but test at forty minutes by inserting a straw into the center part of the cake. If it comes out clean, the cake is done.

When the cake is done, remove it from the oven and allow it to cool for ten minutes. Take it out of the pan, remove the paper, put on a raised grill or rack, and cool for at least two hours before serving.

Add the granulated sugar to the cream and whip just until firm. Put in the bowl from which you will serve it and keep chilled in the refrigerator.

To serve: Slice the cake and place the slices in overlapping fashion on a platter. Take the cream from the refrigerator and shave the chilled chocolate on top of the cream. To shave the chocolate, hold the bar with a paper towel and with a sharp knife, and a light sweeping motion, shave the chocolate into thin curls. This may be done sparingly or lavishly, depending on how you like it. Most people seem to prefer a good deal of chocolate.

OEUFS À LA NEIGE AU CARAMEL

Oeufs à la neige au caramel, a French classic, is elegant in appearance, easy to make, inexpensive, and convenient to serve—which is as much as one can ask of a recipe. It is a specialty of one of the best—and most expensive—restaurants in New York.

INGREDIENTS FOR SIX OR SEVEN

6 egg whites, well beaten

2 cups confectioners sugar

6 egg yolks

2 cups milk

½ vanilla bean, split lengthwise

1¾ cups granulated sugar

1 Tbsp water

To make: Beat the egg whites until they are quite firm, adding the confectioners sugar a bit at a time during the beating. Bring the milk with one-half a vanilla bean to a boil, reduce the heat, and begin poaching the "eggs" (egg whites), which are best formed by using two tablespoons. As closely as possible, they should be symmetrically egg-shaped. Cook only as many at a time as will fit easily, with some room, on the surface of the milk. After two minutes, turn the "eggs" over and continue cooking until they are firm. When one batch is done, remove the "eggs" with a perforated spoon and place them on a linen towel. When they are all cooked, strain the milk and return it to the pot. Beat the egg yolks with three-fourths cup sugar, add the mixture slowly to the milk, and begin making a *crème anglaise* over low heat, stirring constantly until the cream coats the spoon. The sauce should not be too thick.

There is one thing to remember in making this most useful of dessert sauces: if the heat is too high, it will irrevocably spoil the sauce. Amateurs for the most part

[261]

refuse to believe that anything can cook, even at low heat, for the length of time necessary to make this sauce, without something happening. Well, if you make this error and raise the heat, you will find that things happen very quickly indeed; the eggs will curdle and you will have had it. Just be patient. How often I have seen Alice Toklas—whose favorite this sauce was—standing, patiently stirring, and clearly enjoying the delicate process. Chill the *crème anglaise* well, add the "eggs," and return the dish to the refrigerator.

Make the caramel by cooking one cup of sugar with the tablespoon of water over medium heat without stirring. Cook until the sugar is a uniform not-too-dark caramel color. This operation too is touchy, because it takes a very short time for sugar that is at the caramel stage to carbonize—that is, burn.

To serve: Dribble the caramel over the eggs in the *crème anglaise* and serve immediately or after further chilling.

Note: Instead of the caramel you can, as a variation, sprinkle the eggs with very finely slivered and grilled almonds. It is best to buy whole peeled almonds and sliver them yourself. The slivered almonds sold in a package are too coarse; you should be aiming for flavor and not too much texture.

SCHNEEKNODEL WITH FRESH RASPBERRIES

The *schneeknodel* in itself is a quite satisfactory dessert, much esteemed in Austria. I prefer my version; the contrast between the warm, soufflé-like peaks and the chilled raspberries is rather special.

INGREDIENTS FOR FOUR

7 egg whites

2 egg yolks

2 Tbsp sugar

2 Tbsp flour

½ cup vanilla sugar (Put ½ cup confectioners sugar into a jar with ½ a vanilla bean, sliced in two, and set aside for at least two days. The vanilla bean can be used for several batches of vanilla sugar.)

1 quart fresh raspberries, quickly washed and drained

4 Tbsp finely granulated sugar

To make: Preheat the oven to 400°. Separate the whites from the yolks. *It is absolutely essential that not one bit of yolk falls into the whites.* One speck of yolk will prevent the whites from mounting—which, essentially, is what this recipe is about. Beat the yolks until they are lemon colored. Clean the beater very well. Then beat the egg whites until firm but not stiff, adding the two tablespoons of sugar when the whites start to get firm. With a rubber spatula or a large spoon gently fold the egg yolks and flour into the beaten whites, a bit at a time. Butter a large baking sheet— the sort one uses for cookies—and carefully pile the mixture onto it in three peaked mounds. Cook in a 400° oven for from twelve to fifteen minutes. The top of the egg mixture should be brown, but not too much. While the *schneeknodel* is cooking, sprinkle the raspberries with the finely granulated sugar and distribute evenly on a large platter. When the *schneeknodel* is done, with a spatula lift it off the cookie tin in three parts, if possible, and place them on top of the raspberries as attractively as possible.

To serve: Sprinkle the browned egg mixture with the one-half cup vanilla (confectioners) sugar and serve.

TURINOIS

Chestnut desserts tend to be heavy, and *Turinois* could hardly be termed reducing. Since the flavor is inimitable and delicious, however, there is no reason why it cannot be served in small portions. A true dessert should not be a matter of bulk; it should succeed in bringing a meal to a close in as subtle a fashion as possible. I say *close* rather than *climax* because in a properly structured meal the climax is the entrée, which should be led up to and developed away from. I do not mean that the desserts should be anticlimactic, but that the fireworks should become less dazzling without any diminishment of style. An ever-so-perfect raspberry soufflé cannot hope to compete with, say, a perfectly roasted capon with truffles, except in quality.

INGREDIENTS FOR SIX

1 lb can pureed chestnuts (The kind usually available is imported from France and of very good quality. If the pureed chestnuts are sweetened, do not add sugar. If they are not sweetened, mix in 1 cup vanilla sugar—confectioners sugar which has been kept in a closed jar with ½ a vanilla bean, sliced lengthwise, for at least two days.)

3½ ounces butter

3½ ounces unsweetened chocolate

To make: Heat the pureed chestnuts in a double boiler, but don't cook. When they are heated through, remove the top section of the double boiler from the hot water and set aside. Add the butter and chocolate to the chestnuts and let them melt. Stir and mix well. Put the mixture in whatever mold (it should be simple and have a flat bottom) you wish, but put a piece of waxed paper on the bottom to facilitate unmolding. Chill the mold in the freezer part of the refrigerator overnight, but move it to the regular part of the refrigerator at least one hour before serving. Otherwise the *Turinois* will be as hard as a brick and impossible to slice.

To serve: Unmold the *Turinois* on a plate and serve in slices. I like to coat it with whipped cream and sprinkle with crumbled French *gaufrettes* (miniature, very fine, crisp crêpes imported from Brittany, which can usually be found in good shops everywhere).

Note: If you cannot find canned chestnut puree, make your own when chestnuts are available. You will need about one and one-half pounds of uncooked chestnuts. Make a circular cut around each chestnut, put them in water, and bring the water to a boil. Throw the chestnuts into a colander and drain. Peel when they are just cool enough to handle, making sure to remove the skins as well as the shells. As you peel and skin them, throw the chestnuts into another pot of boiling water. Cook until they are soft, which will take about thirty minutes, but test for softness before mashing them with a potato-masher. Then proceed as indicated above, but don't forget the vanilla sugar.

CULINARY
NOTES

Tomatoes

Always use ripe tomatoes for cooking and always peel
and seed them (the skin of a tomato is indigestible and
its seeds are acid). To peel tomatoes, drop them into
boiling water for twenty seconds, remove, and chill in
cold water. The skin can then be removed easily. To
seed, cut the tomatoes in half and, firmly but not
roughly, squeeze the halves until all the seeds have

been forced out. If you want tomatoes with a minimum of acid, sprinkle the cut sides of the peeled and seeded halves with salt, put them cut-side down on a plate, and allow them to drain for twenty minutes. With ripe tomatoes treated in this way, you can make a delicate sauce totally unlike ordinary tomato sauces both in flavor and texture.

Tomato Sauce

Of all the sauces in the American cuisine, the most abused is tomato sauce. I might note that a good deal of it tastes like canned tomato soup, but the observation can hardly have much point since that is precisely what much of it is based on—at least, if I am to believe the women's magazines. Italians—especially Southern Italians—use a great deal of tomato in sauces, but, as anyone who has traveled in Italy knows, all the sauces there are not made with vast quantities of canned tomatoes or tomato paste. In fact, the best chefs in Italy use tomato sparingly; and they use fresh tomatoes, peeled and seeded, which produce a very delicate sauce which enhances rather than masks foods.

The French, to whom the tomato is anything but an all-purpose vegetable, treat it sparingly and carefully, utilizing its acidity and color with great finesse, as in *sole à la Duglère*. This famous Parisian dish would be easy to reproduce in America if channel sole were available—fresh, that is—but the same preparation can be used with fish that are available: fillets of gray sole, flounder, red snapper, and striped bass. (The recipe for *sole à la Duglère* is given on p. 93.) Another example of how the French handle tomatoes is the sautéed chicken called *poulet Celestine* (see p. 101).

Parsley

For its flavoring and blending qualities in food mixtures, the flat, leafy type of parsley called Chinese or
Mexican (*cilantro*) is excellent. For garnishing a dish,
the curly variety is best because it is less likely to
stick to the food. Wash, dry, and store it in the
refrigerator, well wrapped in a damp towel.

Lemons

Of all available natural flavorings, I consider the lemon
to be the finest and most useful. Lemon juice and the
zest (the yellow part of the skin) of lemon lift a dish
in a way nothing else can. Nothing more need be said
about its efficacy and finesse than that lemon is indis-
pensable on caviar and oysters, two of the finest items
on any menu. Lemon also goes very well with jellied
pigs' feet.

Golden Delicious Apples

Most people do not realize what a fine cooking apple
the golden delicious is. Unlike the red delicious, which
is an excellent eating apple but dry and pulpy when
cooked, the golden delicious is ideal for cooking—juicy
with a perfect flavor and texture. Applesauce made
with golden delicious apples, especially when stewed
or lightly mashed but not pureed, has a flavor rather
like pineapple. Because of improved storage methods,
golden delicious apples are now available all year
round.

Scallions

To me, the scallion is the most useful item of produce
stock. Like the shallot, which it somewhat resembles,
the scallion is neither onion nor garlic, but something
nicely in between. It has qualities that other members
of the onion family do not have: It "melts," virtually
dissolving during cooking; it can be eaten raw without
hazard; its green parts make a colorful garnish; and
its cooked flavor is never harsh. In addition, scallions
can be bought the year round. I couldn't do without
them.

Onions

Cooked onion is so ubiquitous in French cooking that
one might begin almost any recipe with the instruction
to peel an onion. However, avoid half-cooked onions as
you would the plague; they are not digestible. If, as in
a meat loaf, there is a good possibility that the onions
won't be thoroughly cooked when the meat is done,
sauté the onions before mixing them into the meat or
use very fine grated onion. People are always attempting—and quite unsuccessfully, I might say—to cook
onions on a spit with meat, as in shashlik and shish
kebab. In Russian Georgia where shashlik originated,
raw scallions are actually chopped and sprinkled over
the meat, rather as the Chinese do with certain of their
dishes. It is something of a bonus that recent research
has proved onions to be a specific against the ill effects
of too much fat in foods. The Hungarians made a
similar discovery: They were addicted to the consumption of paprika (and I don't believe anything
could have induced them to change their ways, least of

all medical advice), but lo-and-behold, someone went to the trouble to prove that paprika is rich in vitamin C.

Anchovies

People have no idea how savory anchovies can be. This is not surprising since very few people are familiar with anything but the canned variety, which, although usually of good quality, is a bit too pungently salty. I prefer—as do the chefs in the Mediterranean countries— the variety that comes in very large jars and is sold in bulk. These are more trouble, of course, because they must be soaked in milk or water to rid them of their excess salt. They must also be boned and skinned, although this is easily done. Apply slight pressure with your fingers, and each anchovy will separate into four fillets, the head, and the bones. Wipe the silvery skin off the fillets and they are ready to use. An advantage of this type of anchovy is its low cost. If the markets you normally patronize do not have this variety, search out Italian, Greek, or Spanish shops. Failing this, for cooking purposes you can always fall back on the usual canned variety, washed and soaked before use.

Olive Oil

I have heard all the arguments, pro and con, about olive oil, and I'm still for it. One argument against olive oil—that it is expensive—is particularly amusing. Everything is relative, of course, but in a country in which people will pay as high as eighty-nine cents a pound for inferior tomatoes, the argument is thin. I have also heard people say, "It's all very well, but I don't like the flavor of olive oil." I have served potatoes sautéed in olive oil to some of these people, and they have invariably remarked favorably on them, assuming they had been cooked in butter. Now when I say I like olive oil, I mean I like olive oil of good quality, preferably from the south of France. (Apropos the question of quality, I have had experiences with misunderstandings. I once took pains to clearly explain a very good recipe for an apple soufflé to an acquaintance—a slight acquaintance, I am glad to say. When I saw her sometime later, she said, "That recipe wasn't very good. Of course, I didn't use very good apples." Another acquaintance to whom I had given the simple recipe for sautéed veal with Marsala wine said, after trying it, "The recipe was not a success—however, I used cooking sherry; perhaps that had something to do with it." This reminds me of Schönberg's remark about his music: "My music is not really so modern, it's just that it's badly played.")

Heating Food Over Steam

Avoid heating food over steam. Recently a professional study found that nothing does a better job of killing the flavor of food than a steam table—thus confirming what good cooks knew all along.

Chilling Stew Overnight

Chilling a stew, or any other dish with meat and a sauce, facilitates removing the fat, which will congeal on the surface. Since a good deal of the flavor in any meat dish is in the fat, it is advantageous to allow the

clear liquid to remain in contact with the fat during
the chilling process, thus absorbing much of the flavor
that would otherwise be lost if the fat were skimmed
off immediately after the dish was cooked. Reheat a
chilled meat dish slowly. Do not bring it to a boil or
the meat will be stringy and, with the last vestiges of
flavorful fat drawn from the meat, the sauce will again
be greasy.

Washing Salad Greens

Iceberg head lettuce, which is so appropriately named
—it has all the flavor of ice—usually doesn't need washing, but other lettuces, such as Bibb and Simpson, do.
For nutritional reasons, washing should be done as
quickly as possible, preferably in a large bowl or pot
filled with cold water. The greens should then be
drained very well. The best way to get rid of the
excess water is to use a salad basket—a wire-net con-
traption with handles to shake and swing until the
salad is dry. Salad baskets are available in shops that
sell imported utensils and appliances; they are inexpensive and, when not in use, are good for storing
onions. To use a salad basket with impunity, however,
it is best to have a terrace or to live in the country,
where you are not likely to spray the local citizens. If
you live in what is known as a modern apartment, with
a New York-type modern kitchen—a closet with appliances—you can put the washed salad in a linen
towel, make sure all apertures are closed, and with a
downward, thrusting motion aimed at the sink, ac-
complish the desired purpose. Then transfer the greens
to a bowl and finish drying them with paper towels.
Cover the bowl with clear plastic wrap and keep it
chilled until just before serving.

Salads

The general rule for salad greens is to break them up rather than cut or slice them. It is a good rule, but I make exceptions, especially with regard to escarole and chicory. At best they are not too tender, but their excellent flavor is most successfully brought out when they are finely chopped or sliced into a *chiffonade* (very thin strips). Try this, for example: Place well-formed, large Boston or Simpson lettuce leaves in a round, fairly deep dish to form a sort of bowl. Chop some chicory very fine and mix it with escarole, slightly less finely chopped, and six extremely finely chopped scallions. Add oil, lemon or vinegar, salt, and pepper; mix again. Put this mixture on the lettuce leaves in a dome, leaving about an inch of the lettuce leaves for a border. Slice a good-sized tomato into eight or nine wedges and fit them, skin-side out, around the edge of the mixed greens. If you like, sprinkle the salad with the well-chopped yolk of a hard-boiled egg.

Croutons

Croutons may mean small cubes, fairly large triangles, or trimmed rounds of sautéed bread. This information wouldn't be worth mentioning if it weren't that some people think croutons, especially the triangles and rounds, may be grilled or toasted. A piece of toast or grilled bread is more absorbent than a blotter and, what is more, on contact with liquid will disintegrate into mush. A dyed-in-the-wool crouton, sautéed in butter or oil, will keep its shape at least long enough to fulfill its function, which is to provide texture and structure. A *tournedos Rossini*, regardless of how thick it has been sliced from the *filet*, looks more imposing with its slice of *foie gras* and truffles when it has been placed on a crouton.

Cayenne Pepper

Despite its innocent tan-orange hue, cayenne pepper is as hot as the hinges of hell, which is precisely why it is so useful. Not only hot, it is pervasive in a way no other pepper is. Although it is at its best in sauces for seafood and chicken, especially when combined with lemon juice, it can contribute a great deal to a wide variety of dishes. In fact, it is most effective when its presence is not suspected—a sign that it has been properly employed. The natural heat of cayenne pepper combined with its interesting flavor can lift an otherwise mundane dish. But anything approaching a heavy hand with this incipiently violent spice can only lead to disaster. Try it a tiny bit at a time, and you will discover where it belongs.

Allowing a Roast to Rest

A roast, whether of beef, lamb, pork, chicken, or turkey, just taken from the oven defies proper carving. Immediate carving results in rubbery meat, and the juice ends up in the platter instead of remaining in the meat where it belongs. The rule, then, for a roast of five pounds is to allow it to rest for at least fifteen minutes before carving or slicing it. If you use a meat thermometer, take the roast from the oven just before it reaches the desired temperature. Good restaurants have warming ovens and special warming receptacles (I don't mean steam tables) for keeping a roast warm. To improvise, set the roast on the open door of the oven with the heat at 200°, hang a sheet of wide, heavy aluminum foil from the top of the oven to cover the oven opening and the roast, and tuck the bottom edge of the sheet of foil under the roast pan or platter. The sheet of foil may be used again and again.

Garnishes

Americans tend to put too much on a plate, and the combinations are sometimes very odd indeed. Although it is perhaps an indication of how I arrange my life, I have been served salad with chow mein, applesauce with beef stew, and grilled steak with sweet potatoes. There is nothing wrong with these combinations, I suppose—if you like them. But there is the tradition of combining foods that have a certain affinity, that complement one another. As Alice Toklas pointed out in her cookbook, the French, having established a good many of the classic food combinations, tend to be rigid, while our combinations lean toward the exotic and even the bizarre. Nowadays, for example, to transform any dish into something-or-other Hawaiian, one merely adds pineapple. Years ago, having noted this development, I foolishly made the remark that we could look forward to what I thought would be the ultimate in instant Hawaiianization—Hawaiian spaghetti. A few days after this foolhardy remark, a recipe for Hawaiian spaghetti appeared in the Sunday supplement of a well-known New York newspaper. This, of course, is more amusing than painful.

On a somewhat higher level, I object to such combinations as steak with rice, *boeuf bourguignon* with rice instead of boiled potatoes, and fresh corn with anything other than a clam bake. Nothing goes so well with steak as potatoes, and no potato garnish is more appropriate than one of the varieties of French fried potatoes. Baked potatoes also go well with steak, but even this felicitous combination becomes warped when served as one restaurant advertises it: "Steak with our one-pound Idaho baked potato." For the love of God, who wants a garnish of one pound of any kind of potatoes.

Apples for Pies or Tartes

Whether intended for a covered pie or sliced for an open *tarte* (see p. 237), the chopped or sliced apples should be put in a bowl, sprinkled with sugar, and set aside for an hour. The sugar will draw some of the liquid from the apples, considerably reducing the possibility of bubbling-over pies and a smoked-up kitchen. This also eliminates what some consider the necessity of sprinkling the apples with flour to thicken the juice. Of course, the liquid drawn from the apples is not thrown away. It is reduced over medium heat until it has thickened to a glaze, which is added to a covered pie after it has been taken from the oven and cooled somewhat. Pour the glaze into the pie through a paper funnel inserted in one of the slashes of the crust or through the paper chimney, if you use one. For an open *tarte*, mix the apple juice with apricot jelly and cook until it is thoroughly smooth and reduced to a glaze. Brush this over the crust and apple slices of the *tarte* ten minutes before it is done.

Buying Meat

Although there are still a few butchers who know their trade and are willing to work at it, nowadays many of us must buy our meat at supermarkets. This has its hazards, not the least of which is the necessity of learning to cope with a host of hitherto unknown cuts, especially of beef. For example, I have seen so many different cuts of chuck beef, each with its own peculiar name, that I believe there must be young and inexperienced shoppers who think that chuck is the name of a special breed of cattle. This isn't as farfetched as it sounds; since the same young and inexperienced shoppers never see fillet of beef in the supermarkets—although they see all sorts of spurious fillets, including, I am sure, fillet of chuck—they must assume that there is a breed of cattle without fillets. That the sides of beef supermarkets buy do arrive in the store with fillets is revealed from time to time by the rather furtive appearance among the other cuts of beef of clumsy-looking lumps, tapered at one end, which are labeled *filet mignon*. This, of course, is the accurate term for the tapered ends of fillets of beef, which doesn't explain, but helps one to surmise, what happened to the rest of the fillets. Also, since these ends of the fillets are not trimmed of the heavy layer of fat which covers them, *mignon* (delicately pretty) is not exactly the adjective for them. Clearly, if you must have fillet of beef (for beef Stroganoff or beef Wellington, for example), it is advisable to buy it in a reputable butcher shop.

Aside from the matter of familiar and unfamiliar cuts, there is the more serious problem of how to handle meat that is generally clammy and overmoist. It is impossible to sauté crisply, grill, or roast meat that has not been hung long enough or to do anything worthwhile with frozen chicken until it has been thoroughly thawed and allowed to dry. And drying chicken with paper towels won't help; in fact, the paper towels will repeatedly draw the moisture to the surface, and since the moisture is the meat's juices, there won't be much flavor left. What must be done is to remove the cellophane wrapper, wipe the meat with a clean cloth, wrap it loosely in waxed paper with the pieces separated from one another, and store in the refrigerator for at least twelve hours. Do not put the wrapped meat on a plate; put it directly on a wire grill in the moderately cold part of the refrigerator. This procedure isn't absolutely necessary in the case of meats for stewing or braising, although it facilitates the browning process that usually precedes the addition of water or other liquids. (When browning meat, as is customary for a sauté [see p. 99], do not crowd the pan or you will discover just how much liquid there really is in the meat as well as the fact that the liquid prevents browning. Brown a few pieces, remove them to a plate, and continue until all the meat is browned.)

Buying Wines

I have been asked many times how one learns about wines. It is a good question because implicit in it is the realization that there is something to learn. My answer, which is not mean to be discouraging but merely realistic, is to spend a lot of money and drink a lot of wine. I do not mean to suggest that you have to become a wino, but that tasting, not reading, is the only path to true knowledge. Nevertheless, a good book on wines *can* save you a lot of money and time and help you to avoid some nasty experiences. To those young people who are always asking whether absolute values exist, I would answer yes: a bottle of Chateau Mouton Rothschild of a good year, properly aged under ideal conditions, is a great wine, whether it tastes good to you or not. At the other end of the scale, I would consider it wise to discover what does taste good to you by trying lesser but honest wines, not forgetting that everything from there is up. Eventually your discrimination will become established.

Shapes and Flavors

It's curious, but the way vegetables are shaped, meat is sliced, salad is broken, and even bread is cut affects their flavors. The best example of this is pasta. I don't know how many varieties of pasta there are, but regardless of the number (when correctly cooked and served with their appropriate sauces or, as with *fettucini*, merely with butter and cheese), they are all remarkably individual in flavor. In the south of France, where Italian influence is strong, there is even a special type of pasta for fish soup. As another example, there is a correct way to prepare a cucumber sandwich: Very thinly sliced cucumber is placed between thin slices of buttered white bread from which the crust has been trimmed; the sandwich is then cut into strips.

Just thinking about the correctness of such a teatime delicacy takes me on the rebound to the memory of a very different sort of sandwich—a *casse-croûte* I had in Senlis, a beautiful cathedral village not far from Paris. I was hungry, so hungry that I felt I simply must eat—

a rare compulsion for me. Since Senlis at that time was
not the sort of village to boast of a snack shop if it had
one (which it did not) and since it was neither lunch
nor dinner time, I went into a most ordinary appearing
café-tabac and asked the proprietor if he could produce
something in the shape of food. He could, he said,
give me a sandwich of pâté, but as he was not a pro-
tagonist of the hard-sell school, I got the impression
that he was offering me some sort of commercial pâté.
Nevertheless, I ordered a sandwich as well as a glass
of red wine. Well, that was some snack. The sandwich,
which was about the size of a football, consisted of
also excellent, was the best snack by far I have ever
tasted, set between two halves of the crustiest bread
imaginable, well spread with butter—real butter, not the
cold storage kind. This sandwich along with the wine,
also excellent, was the best snack by far I have ever
enjoyed, in France or anywhere else. But when I ex-
pressed my enthusiasm for what I regarded as a fortu-
itous bounty, the proprietor said something to the effect
that good food was everyone's due. I wish more people
felt that way.

Rosemary

I treat this herb separately because it is the most difficult of all to handle. The phrase "sprinkle with rosemary" sounds nice, but, as Elizabeth David pointed
out in her wonderful book *French Provincial Cooking*,
it is a nasty experience to get one of the needles (they
do resemble pine needles) in your mouth: You don't
want to chew it, you can't swallow it, so you remove it
and put it on the plate. Aside from the fact that rosemary is far too pungent to handle in an offhand way,
using the needles on grilled meat or fish (with which

it goes well) only makes sense if you distribute them fairly evenly, which usually means more rosemary than anyone wants. My solution is to put as many needles as you wish into a pepper grinder (I have one of those admirable Peugot grinders with a handle) and grind it over whatever you wish to roast or grill. The flavor will be fresh, as powdered herbs rarely are, and will require only a little rosemary. Try it on a leg of lamb, a rib roast of beef, a grilled red snapper, or a veal roast basted with white wine.

Odors

If you are cooking cabbage and your family and the neighbors are aware of it, you are not cooking it correctly, or, to be specific, you are cooking it over too high heat. The same applies to roasting meat at too high a temperature. In roasting a chicken, the fat and juices in the pan should never be darker than a light tan. When shrimp are boiled instead of poached, they are unpleasantly odiferous and, of course, will be mushy in texture and without flavor. Shrimp should be thrown into boiling water, the water brought back just to the boil again, and then simmered over low heat— the length of time depending on the size of the shrimp. The proper way to poach fish—salmon, say—is in a court bouillon (a prepared stock—see p. 96) that is just apparently simmering (in other words, with virtually no surface agitation of the liquid). Cooked this way, fish has a superb taste and texture with no odor. Another example of flavor lost through overcooking is the much vaunted camp coffee that smells so appetizing in the open air and tastes so flat when you get around to drinking it. The Turks, who know a thing or two about coffee, cook it in a pot that, while quite wide at the bottom, tapers in sharply at the top. (These pots are available in large cities, but any glass or enameled pot will do just as well.) They add water and coffee (two tablespoons of coffee to one measuring cup of water), bring them to a boil, and, just before it foams over, take the pot off the heat. The coffee is then brought to a foaming boil two more times with about thirty seconds wait in between. After the third boiling the coffee is served immediately, poured through a fine sieve into cups. If first-quality coffee is used, this method invariably produces excellent coffee of the sort Americans like. To avoid possible confusion, this is not what is generally known as Turkish coffee, which is a sort of dense puree of pulverized coffee, water, and sugar—to my taste, a little much.

Excess Fat

No chef worthy of the name would consider serving a sauté of chicken, or any other dish with sauce, without first removing the excess fat—95 percent of whatever oil, butter, or animal fats rise to the surface of a sauce. Yet I have read countless recipes in which the subject was completely ignored. If these recipes are followed to the letter, as I presume some of them are, a good many people must be eating some very greasy food. More than likely, though, good sense prevails, and the excess fat is disposed of as it should be, by carefully spooning it off the surface and rejecting it. Another, and easier, method of removing the fat is to chill the entire cooked dish in the utensil it was cooked in. This will congeal the fat, which can then be lifted off with a perforated spoon.

The very term *excess fat* implies that there is other fat that is *not* in excess. The implication is correct. The bulk of the flavor in meat dishes resides in the fat; it is therefore imperative that a small amount remain on the surface of the sauce—about 5 percent, as indicated above. In short, fat is not to be despised, but rather utilized for its flavor and its function of nourishing lean meat and keeping it tender and juicy. It must then be removed and rejected—the excess, that is—because of its indigestibility.

Truffles

The aroma of a fresh truffle, immersed in cognac or whiskey, will pervade a large room. The aroma of a canned truffle—the truffle removed from the can and similarly immersed in cognac or whiskey—will be only faintly noticeable a few feet away. Since a truffle loses so much during the canning process and the canned variety is the only sort to be had in America, should we bother with them at all? I would say yes. Canned truffles (and some brands are better than others, so try various brands) with their flavor, which is inimitable, their texture, also inimitable, and their striking color enhance pâtés, delicately sautéed veal, chicken, and egg dishes as no substitute can. If I am going to eat a *tournedos Rossini* (a sautéed slice of fillet of beef, set on a crouton fried in butter, crowned with a slice of *foie gras* and a hefty slice of truffle on top), I want the truffle—fresh or canned.

I wonder if anyone has attempted to freeze-dry truffles. A dried mushroom or morel has more flavor than the fresh—less delicate, but beautifully pungent. Incidentally, the freeze-drying process is in a high state of development in France, which is where the truffles are.

Reheating Leftover Meat

The simple rule for reheating leftover meat is to avoid overheating. This does not mean that it must be served half-cold; leftovers can be heated to the point at which they are palatably hot (many degrees lower than most people realize).

If you feel that this information is too far beneath your culinary interests, allow me to remind you that Escoffier took considerable pains to explain this principle. Here it is—and I advise you to try it at least once. You have, say, a good-sized piece of roast of beef which, for one reason or another, you don't wish to use for sandwiches or hash. You want to serve it for lunch or for dinner, but don't want it to taste like leftovers. Take the meat out of the refrigerator and set it aside until it reaches room temperature. Remove any fat from the surface of the leftover sauce or gravy, reject it, and put the sauce in a pot. Add a can of beef bouillon and reduce the mixture by one-third by boiling it over high heat. (If there is no sauce or gravy left, simply use the bouillon and reduce it.) In the meantime, slice the beef very thin and trim off all fat and gristle. When the bouillon is at the correct density, follow this sequence: Turn off the heat under the bouillon to stop the boiling, add a few slices of the beef, and, after about thirty seconds, drain them. Serve the beef, with a tablespoon of bouillon over it, on a heated plate accompanied by mashed potatoes with butter. For each serving repeat the sequence of bringing the bouillon to the boil, turning off the heat, immersing the slices of beef, and draining them. Believe it or not, the beef will taste like the real thing. Although all meats may be reheated in this way, it perhaps works best with ham.

Cheese

An aphorism of Brillat-Savarin, the French gastronom-ist, is: "Dessert without cheese is like a pretty girl with only one eye." I don't feel that strongly on the subject because I think the role of cheese depends on how the meal is composed. In a not-too-formal meal, especially one consisting of robust courses, I believe cheese can be dispensed with, but for a subtly designed meal of some formality, served with proper wines, I feel a cheese course is imperative. The French, who are masters of menu-planning, go to great pains to assure that the best wine is served with the cheese, which says all that has to be said about its rank in their culinary galaxy. However, the best cheeses are alive and, like wines, arrive at one peak of perfection, after which they decline—and rapidly. Nothing is more disappoint-ing to the palate than a good cheese—a Brie, for ex-ample—which has passed its prime. To learn to select cheeses, find a reliable shop and begin developing—through taste, sight, and, in the case of soft-ripening cheeses, feel—an idea of what cheeses should be.

Gruyère and other non-soft-ripening cheeses should be kept in the refrigerator until just before they are served; otherwise they sweat and taste oily. Soft-ripened cheeses should be served at room temperature and at their peak. A Camembert bought by the slice, which consists of two chalky layers with a thin, soft interior, will not be worth eating. A properly handled Brie (my favorite cheese) is soft and creamy through-out and light in color—and not easy to come by. A cheese that is almost always safe is Roquefort, but, since it too is quite alive, it must be bought at peak (before it begins to take on a brownish tinge).

Cheeses in restaurants are rarely good because they —the cheeses, that is—must travel a good deal between the dining room and the refrigerator. The better restaurants now concentrate on offering a few very fine cheeses, which, in my opinion, is a good way to handle a rather difficult item. Good cheese is expensive. I have never been satisfied with a restaurant's so-called cheese board, which more often than not looks like the detritus of a careless housekeeper's refrigerator.

Mushrooms

The cultivated mushroom available the year round is a most useful vegetable. (Technically the mushroom is a cryptogam, but for the purpose of this book I shall call it a vegetable.) Buy only firm mushrooms with the underside closed; they should not look like white umbrellas with a black lining. In their raw state mushrooms are best cleaned by careful wiping with a cloth, as they should not be touched by water. They may be peeled or not, depending on the recipe and the appearance of the mushrooms, but there is a great deal of flavor in the peels (large restaurants use them to flavor sauces). The only part of the mushroom discarded is the bottom of the stem, which is usually brownish in color and a trifle tough in texture. If the stems are not used, make a little mushroom essence by cooking them and the peels gently in water with the juice of one-fourth of a lemon for fifteen minutes. Strain the liquid and use it to flavor a sauce or a soup. If the only mushrooms you can buy are not too fresh and have opened, you may have to wash them to get rid of sand or dirt. In that case wash them rapidly in water to which the juice of one-half of a lemon has been added.

Drain them well and dry them in a cloth or paper towels before cooking.

Melons

Alice Toklas used to say that although melons were no doubt very good, she never knew when to serve them. Since her breakfast consisted of two cups of coffee at 5:30 A.M.—the middle of the night to me— she didn't know how refreshing a cool slice of melon could be in the morning, especially on a hot day. And since she didn't like and even disapproved of cured meats, she wasn't interested in that most delicious combination, Prosciutto and melon. However, I noticed that when we lunched at restaurants in the south of France, where melons are so taken for granted they are automatically included in the *hors d'oeuvre varié*, Alice ate her portion without demur. (I suppose this could be attributed to the air and ambience of Provence, which even succeeded in convincing Alice in her seventieth year that soup had its merits. On one occasion after her conversion to soup, we almost missed the train from Cannes because she wouldn't leave until she had had one more bowl of *soupe de poisson*, the pungent fish soup so characteristic of the Côte d'Azur.)

The difficulty with melons is determining a good one. This isn't easy. Alexandre Dumaine (one of the greatest living chefs, now retired) used to take the time to go to the market in Saulieu and personally select the melons for his restaurant. He spent valuable time going through a ritual that, believe it or not, is effective—at least for Dumaine. How does he select melons? Well, first he hefts them and then taps them with his forefinger to determine by feel and sound whether the melons are plumply full or hollow and spare. Then he sniffs the stem ends for aroma and presses them to see if they respond to pressure as they should; he inspects them closely to see if they have the *couronne*, or crown —a circle of slightly lighter (actually faded) skin around the stem, which indicates that a melon is ripe. Finally, and only after some reflection and several sighs, he sets certain melons aside as adequate.

Having revealed the secrets of this ritual, do I believe I have substantially lessened the difficulty of choosing a melon? I do not. However, there are shops that sell the more expensive, usually large melons—such as honeydew, Cranshaw, Spanish, and Persian—by the half, quarter, or slice, and the more amiable shopkeepers will offer a sliver as a sample. This helps.

The best way to serve a good melon is chilled and plain, in slices, although it is not a foolish refinement to cut out a wedge some three inches wide from one side, remove the seeds with a long-handled spoon, and fill the melon with good, not-too-sweet, imported (in other words, genuine) port wine. Replace the wedge, chill the melon for at least two hours, and serve it in scoops using a sharp-edged spoon, adding some wine to each serving. This is a particularly good way to serve a large Cranshaw melon.

Cucumbers, Eggplant, Zucchini

Cucumbers, eggplant, and zucchini, despite their succulence, have little food value; food value and calories are usually laid on in the form of oil, cheese, bread crumbs, or tomato sauce. All three contain a high percentage of water, eggplant has a certain bitterness, and zucchini and cucumbers have a substance that provokes what is euphemistically known as "repeating." The wateriness, the bitterness, and the "repeating" characteristic can be easily rectified by peeling and slicing the vegetables or by merely slicing them and sprinkling the cut surfaces with salt. In thirty minutes a good deal of water will have drained from the vegetables. After sponging and drying with paper towels, eggplant and zucchini are ready for cooking. With cucumbers it is better to pour off the accumulated liquid, sprinkle with salt again, cover with water, and set aside for an hour more—or even all night, in which case the cucumbers should be refrigerated to prevent fermentation.

Obviously, if you peel and slice the vegetables and blanch them in boiling salted water, the above procedure isn't necessary; but because the textures will be quite different, the vegetables must be used in different preparations. For instance, after salting, soaking, and draining, cucumbers are served cold with a vinaigrette or sour cream dressing; after blanching in boiling water, they are gently cooked in butter and served as a garnish. A specialty of one of the great three-star restaurants in Paris is capon with sautéed cucumbers.

INDEX

[**291**]